Twayne's Filmmakers Series

Warren French

EDITOR

Roger Corman

Roger Corman. Photograph by Sarah Quill.

Roger Corman

GARY MORRIS

BOSTON

Twayne Publishers

1985

Dedicated to my parents,
Fred and Elaine,
with love

Roger Corman

is first published in 1985 by Twayne Publishers,
A Division of G. K. Hall & Company
All Rights Reserved

Book Production by Elizabeth Todesco

Printed on permanent/durable acid-free paper and bound
in the United States of America.

First Printing, 1985

Uncredited stills are from the collection of the author,
former editor of *Bright Lights* magazine

Library of Congress in Publication Data

Morris, Gary.
Roger Corman.

(Twayne's filmmakers series)
Bibliography: p. 153
Filmography: p. 154
Includes index.
1. Corman, Roger, 1926-   —Criticism and interpretation.
I. Title.   II. Series.
PN1998.A3C7865 1985   791.43′0233′0924   85-8483
ISBN 0-8057-9304-6

Contents

About the Author

GARY MORRIS WAS BORN in Glendale, Ohio, in 1951. He combined early interests in literature and publishing by issuing a poetry journal comprised of the work of friends and neighbors at age fourteen. He attended Yale Summer High School in 1967 and 1968, where he studied literature and creative writing.

Morris studied film and literature at Wesleyan University in Middletown, Connecticut, where he received a B.A. in 1973. He wrote film reviews for two years for a newspaper in Cincinnati, as well as program notes for film series at the Hartford Athenaeum and the University of Southern California.

In 1974 he began publishing *Bright Lights*, a film criticism magazine that was the only strictly auteurist publication in America to date. *Bright Lights*, which Morris also edited and designed, published the work of critics like John Belton, Andrew Sarris, and Doug McVay, and is known particularly for a special issue on the films of Douglas Sirk published in conjunction with a retrospective of Sirk's films at the Museum of Modern Art.

His other publications include *StarSet: Automated Phototypesetting System*, in collaboration with Stan De Gulis. He is currently at work on a history of rockabilly.

Editor's Foreword

FOR A LONG TIME before the inception of this series, I had thought it particularly important that an adequate hearing be given to the claims for Roger Corman as an auteurist filmmaker on the basis of the series of often highly sensational, low-budget films that he made between 1955 and 1967, culminating in a cycle based loosely on the writings of Edgar Allan Poe.

Corman's achievement has often been condescendingly dismissed, especially in the United States, because most of the films he directed were "B" productions, made in an incredible three to ten days that did not, because of their production schedules, offer very polished performances. Low-budget filmmaking, however, offers an imaginative, creative filmmaker—for reasons that Gary Morris explains in this book—an unusual opportunity to present his private vision of the world with a minimum of interference from the financial backers who have often become disastrously involved in big-budget productions. The possibilities of these modest films are especially great if the filmmaker happens to strike a responsive note in an alienated public searching for unconventional entertainment.

Corman's work has far more in common with the shoestring productions of independent, underground filmmakers like Kenneth Anger than with the commercial cinema of the dying years of the effort to control and sentimentalize Hollywood's output through a traditional puritanical production code. Corman had the unusual gift, however, of being able to appeal precisely to the tastes and yearnings of disaffected young audiences that frequented particularly the drive-in theaters that thrived on low-budget fare.

The quality of individual performances did not matter much at such showings, for it was difficult to appreciate finely nuanced performances in the monstrously enlarged, diffused image on the open-air screen. The kind of acting appropriate to Victorian melodrama best suited the setting, as the memorable performances of Vincent Price as the archetypal Poe persona proved. Corman's movies were not made for tiny preview rooms or small-screen television.

What mattered at the drive-ins was an ornate style and larger-than-life, often grotesque actions that conveyed emphatically a story that entranced the audiences. Corman's films certainly were—as Gary Morris also illustrates in detail—noteworthy for their mise-en-scène and cinematography, the work of a group of astute collaborators who comprised a continuing stock company.

Behind Corman's films there was, most important of all, what was lacking in most B films, a consistent vision; and it is this vision that Gary Morris explains in greatest detail in this book. By way of preview, it is appropriate only to say that he finds Corman's films generally deal with a corrupt civilization that expresses a wish to self-destruct through "machines of violence." He also illuminates the way in which Corman's films serve as a self-portrait of the creator through the repeated portrayal of a highly intelligent artist working under crassly commercial circumstances.

These characteristics suggest that the most interesting questions that Corman's films pose lie not in their artistry, but in their relationship to the times that produced them and the audiences that consumed them voraciously. What we can learn about the increasingly disaffected, "Beat" world of the late 1950s and early 1960s through Corman's generally apocalyptic visions may open windows on our past.

It was probably no accident that the Poe cycle was both the high point and virtually the conclusion of Corman's career as an auterist director. After completing only three more of his most controversial films—*The Wild Angels, The Trip,* and *The St. Valentine's Day Massacre*—Corman devoted himself to the production and distribution of generally offbeat American and imported films. As Gary Morris points out, over the course of the six films that constitute the core of the Poe cycle, Corman made both more elaborate films with constantly larger budgets and more cautiously optimistic films. He seems to have worked out on the screen through this cycle the problems about human behavior that most bothered him, and he seems to have had little interest in involving himself in the time and financial and managerial problems involved in more ambitious productions. Certainly he quit while he was ahead, as few have had the self-insight to do.

The most remarkable thing about Corman is that there have been so few others like him who have displayed the knack for using the motion picture to achieve such almost unvarying success in sharing a vision with a particular audience at a particular time.

Because of Corman's extraordinary productivity during his scarcely more than a dozen years as a director, it would be impossible to examine in detail all of the forty-eight films he directed. Gary Morris has, therefore, judiciously limited himself to detailed analyses of sixteen of the most popular and most controversial of Corman's work, ten of them illustrative of three principal "genres" in which he achieved some of his greatest successes (though most of his films were actually antigeneric deconstructions of traditional clichés), the other six constituting the Poe cycle.

W. F.

Preface

THIS IS THE FIRST full-length critical study in English of the films of Roger Corman. I have chosen not to engage in a lengthy "justification" of Corman as a significant postwar film artist; as Andrew Sarris said of George Cukor, "His filmography is his best defense." Of course, Corman's case is not quite that simple. His films have gained a place in the collective public mind through initial mass marketing and frequent exposure on television, but Corman has had few champions among the tastemakers of art—the academics and critics who have laid down many of the ground rules for what is "good" and "bad" in the most misunderstood of art forms: film. This lack of defenders has resulted in undue neglect of Corman, and many of his films are now difficult or impossible to see as he shot them. Most of the Poe films are no longer available in 'scope, and many have faded to red. A few of the films, for example, *Rock All Night* and *I, Mobster*, seem to have disappeared entirely. One purpose of this book is to stimulate interest in Corman as creator rather than creative businessman. Corman's role as the patron saint of the "Hollywood New Wave" of the sixties and seventies has obscured his own important contributions as an exemplar of the modernist sensibility to film art.

Because Corman's career encompassed so many films in a relatively brief time (he directed forty-nine features between 1955 and 1970 and has produced perhaps 150 films to date), the problem of how to approach his work arose early. I have arranged the films along thematic lines, attempting to uncover the distinctive thematic and stylistic elements in the films of this most visually oriented director, and to show the astounding internal consistency of his work and the evolution of his worldview from the drab minimalism of his early black-and-white films to the complex nihilism of such later color masterpieces as *X— The Man with the X-Ray Eyes* and *The Tomb of Ligeia*. I have included technical and historical details insofar as they help disclose the internal workings of the films themselves, but generally I have subordinated these elements to thematic/stylistic analysis. This seems particularly apropos in light of two recent books on Corman that extensively detail production circumstances, budgets, and historical background.

I decided at the outset to discuss Corman's most important and/or representative work rather than attempt a comprehensive analysis of his entire career, a project well beyond the scope of this book. In addition, I have focused on Corman's own directorial efforts, with minimal attention given to his productions for AIP, New World, and other companies. While it is certainly important to note that Corman gave first opportunities to such acclaimed modern filmmakers as Martin Scorsese, Monte Hellman, Peter Bogdanovich, Francis Ford Coppola, and others, this book takes the view that Corman is an artist superior to his many protégés, hence the slant toward Corman's own work.

Chapter 1 contains a brief biography and sets up a framework for discussion, placing Corman in the context of the low-budget, independent film and analyzing certain recurring themes, motifs, and stylistic approaches we find in his films. Chapters 2–4 group some of his most important non-Poe films as examples of some of his most persistent subjects and themes. Chapter 5 discusses Corman's greatest achievement, the Poe series, while Chapter 6 discusses certain critical reactions to Corman and some of the reasons behind them.

GARY MORRIS

Acknowledgments

I WISH TO THANK several people whose generosity facilitated the writing of this book. First, my good friend Michael Stern for suggesting I do the book. I am grateful to my editor, Warren French, for arranging the inclusion of Corman in this series, and for kindly maintaining a hands-off posture during the writing. The people at New World Pictures, Corman's former studio, were responsive in arranging interviews and providing information, and Corman himself was unfailingly pleasant and patient in answering my questions.

My friend Jerry Kutner was a major influence on the book. An avid and brilliant student of films and culture, his comments on Corman provided much insight into the director. Jack Foley's extraordinary letters and film articles altered my perception of both writing and film, and I wish to thank him.

My good friend John Tessitore, another Corman devotee, shared ideas and prodded me into finishing the project. For having just the right amount of patience and indulgence, I owe special debts to Gregory Battle and Sylvia Morris. Don McGlynn was kind enough to provide good conversation, often hard-to-find prints, and projection equipment. Steve Buckles uncovered several extremely rare Corman films, and I am grateful. For the use of computer equipment, a thank you to Bennett, Elliott, and Herbert Derman of Graphic Typesetting Service in Los Angeles. A tip of the hat to John Torzilli for his superior proofreading skills (and considerable film knowledge). Final thanks to Lee Sanders for providing me with a copy of *Roger Corman: The Millennic Vision* after mine fell apart.

Chronology

1926   Roger Corman born in Detroit, Michigan, 6 April, son of William and Ann Corman.

1940   Family moves to Beverly Hills, California.

1943   Graduates from Beverly Hills High School.

1947   Graduates from Stanford University with degree in engineering. Spends three years in Navy.

1951   Works as messenger, then story analyst at Twentieth Century-Fox. Studies English literature at Oxford University.

1953   Sells first script to Allied Artists for *Highway Dragnet*.

1954   Becomes silent co-partner in American Releasing Corporation.

1955   Directs *Five Guns West*, *Apache Woman*, *The Day the World Ended*, *Swamp Women*, and *The Oklahoma Woman*. Forms own production company.

1956   *The Gunslinger, It Conquered the World, Not of This Earth, The Undead, Attack of the Crab Monsters*, and *Rock All Night*. Goes to Hawaii to direct *She Gods of Shark Reef* and *Naked Paradise*. ARC becomes American-International Pictures.

1957   *Teenage Doll, Carnival Rock, Sorority Girl, The Viking Women and the Sea Serpent*, and *War of the Satellites*.

1958   *Machine Gun Kelly, Teenage Caveman*, and *I, Mobster*.

1959   *Bucket of Blood* and *The Wasp Woman*.

1960   Starts independent production/distribution company, the Filmgroup. *Ski Troop Attack, The House of Usher*, and *The Little Shop of Horrors*. Shoots *Atlas* in Greece. Shoots *The Last Woman on Earth* and *Creature from the Haunted Sea* back-to-back in Puerto Rico.

1961   *The Pit and the Pendulum*, *The Premature Burial*, and *Tales of Terror*. His independent feature *The Intruder* is denied Motion Picture Code stamp because of the word "nigger." Corman takes the issue to court and wins.

1962   *Tower of London*, *The Young Racers*, and *The Raven*. Releases *The Terror* after two years of on-and-off shooting by Corman, Francis Ford Coppola, and Jack Hill.

1963   *X—The Man with the X-Ray Eyes* and *The Haunted Palace*. Goes to Yugoslavia to shoot *The Secret Invasion*.

1964   French Film Institute offers first retrospective of his work. Goes to England to shoot *The Masque of the Red Death* and *The Tomb of Ligeia*.

1966   *The Wild Angels* is the American entry to the Venice Film Festival, almost causing an international scandal. Shoots *The St. Valentine's Day Massacre*, his most expensive production (Twentieth Century-Fox).

1967   *The Trip* is withdrawn from Cannes as an American entry, but succeeds in domestic release. Begins work on *A Time for Killing* at Columbia but abandons production over "artistic differences."

1969   *Bloody Mama*. Directs only television movie, *What's in It for Harry?* (rejected by ABC as "too violent").

1970   *Gas-s-s-s*. AIP's "butchering" of this film causes Corman to leave AIP and start his own studio, New World Pictures, which specializes in production and distribution of low- and middle-budget independent films, and distribution of prestige foreign films by directors like Truffaut and Fellini. Directs his final film to date, *von Richthofen and Brown*, for United Artists.

1971–1983   Runs New World Pictures and produces a few films for other studios, including Scorsese's *Boxcar Bertha*, Steve Carver's *Capone*, and Bogdanovich's *Saint Jack*.

1983   Corman sells New World and its package of 150-plus films to a group of lawyers, and starts another company, Horizon Pictures, to make "middle-range" independent features.

1

Corman in Context

Biography

ROGER CORMAN WAS BORN in Detroit, Michigan, on 5 April 1926 to William and Ann Corman. The family moved to Beverly Hills, California, while Corman was still a teenager, and he attended Beverly Hills High School and then Stanford University, where he obtained a degree in engineering. "I had this idea in the back of my mind that a son should follow in his father's footsteps," he said, but unlike his father, Corman worked only briefly as an engineer after graduation. Like many future directors, the young Corman was an avid moviegoer, recalling with special fondness the films of John Ford (*My Darling Clementine*) and fantasy efforts like Hal Roach's *One Million B.C.* Indeed, Corman evinced a general interest in fantasy from his earliest youth, that embraced the extremes of popular culture from films to pulp magazines like *Astounding Science Fiction*. Much of his future film work would derive from this early preoccupation, with about half of his films falling into the genres of science fiction and horror.

Corman began what could be considered his creative life during his college days, when he combined practical, technical expertise with self-expression by writing free-lance articles for magazines like *Popular Mechanics* and *Science and Mechanics*. This early experience of earning money through creative ventures—particularly writing—influenced his initial decision to become a writer (his first Hollywood credit is as writer rather than director). He spent three years in the Navy, followed by a semester at Oxford University in England studying English literature. Returning to America, Corman began writing scripts "but no one paid much attention." He got a job as a messenger at Fox and worked his way up to story analyst before selling his first script, "House by the River" to Allied Artists, which retitled it *Highway Dragnet* to capitalize on the popularity of a television show with a similar name. Corman's insistence on receiving an associate producer credit in addition to the writer credit showed his sound business sense and gave him a stronger initial foothold in the industry.

Corman on the set of Bloody Mama (1969). *Courtesy of* Phototeque.

1

In 1954, after producing several low-budget genre films, Corman became the silent third partner in a fledgling low-budget film company, American Releasing Corporation. Resisting offers of employment from Republic and Lippert Studios, Corman agreed to supply the films that James Nicholson, a sales manager for Realart Pictures, and Samuel Arkoff, an industry lawyer, would finance and distribute. Corman's earliest efforts for the company were straightforward genre films—westerns, adventure pictures, science fiction—but his fast and efficient shooting methods (six- to ten-day schedules were the norm) guaranteed profits and Corman was able to set up his own unit that he used not only for American Releasing Corporation—which changed its name to American-International Pictures in 1956—but for films he produced and directed for other studios as well. This unit consisted most frequently of Corman as director/producer, Charles Griffith as writer, Floyd Crosby as cinematographer, and people like Francis Doel as story editor and Chuck Hanawalt as key grip. The group worked so cohesively that it developed a strong reputation around Hollywood, and Corman rented them out to other studios when they were not working for him.

Corman's association with AIP lasted from 1955 to 1969, when he left them to start his own studio, New World Pictures. (A previous attempt, the Filmgroup, lasted from 1960 to 1962 and produced only a handful of films.) Corman was somewhat invisible during the 1950s, but gained widespread prominence beginning in 1960 with a series of films based on the work of Edgar Allan Poe. His rejuvenation of the horror genre—combining his own sensibility with the influence of a series of sensual horror films from Hammer Studios in England (and cross-pollinated with the work of Italian director Mario Bava)—resulted in widespread acclaim. Corman also became controversial during his second decade as a director, with a court battle (over the denial of an MPAA Seal to his racially progressive film, *The Intruder*), a near-scandal (the uproar over the submission of the violent *The Wild Angels* as the American entry at the Venice Film Festival in 1966), and a continuous alienation of the critics with his "endorsement of drugs" (*The Trip*) and his graphic use of violence (*Bloody Mama*). Corman's low profile during the 1950s changed radically in the sixties, and his reputation as a maverick independent earned him several nicknames including "King of the B's" and "Schlockmeister." Like Jerry Lewis, Corman received stronger response in Europe—particularly in France where the French Film Institute held the earliest retrospective of his work in 1964—than in America, where critics tended to see him as a man who recognized the talents of *others*, rather than an artist in his own right. His early use of people like Peter Bogdanovich, Martin

Scorsese, Jack Nicholson, Robert De Niro, and most of what came to be known as "the New Hollywood" solidified this reputation.

In 1970, Corman started New World Pictures, a company he headed until 1983, when he sold it. Corman developed New World as a sort of miniature AIP, though he split its format between producing low-budget genre pictures (*The Big Doll House*) and distributing foreign prestige films like Bergman's *Cries and Whispers* and Fellini's *Amarcord*, a dichotomy that further fixes his reputation as more a patron than an artist.

Corman married one of his assistants, Julie, in 1975, and they have three children. In 1983, Corman started a new company, Millennium Films. The name paid tribute to the first serious book about Corman's films, the Edinburgh Film Festival's *Roger Corman: The Millennic Vision*, a seminal work in the recasting of Corman's place in history as a film artist; but the name was later changed to Horizon Pictures.

Independent Filmmaker

Contrary to popular belief, Corman was not an "AIP director," any more than he could be called an "Allied Artists director" or a "Howco director." There is the general supposition that because AIP and Allied and other companies released films by Corman under their logo that he was under contract to them and used their "studio facilities" in the way that, for example, Frank Borzage could be called an "MGM director" or Allan Dwan a "Republic director" during their tenures at those studios. Certainly, Corman had a strong relationship with AIP and could be considered a founding member in spite of the fact that he was not one of the company's owners. But, except for a brief period in the 1960s, AIP did not even have a studio, but acted primarily as a distributor for films either produced independently and given to them, or funded and then distributed by them.

This is a far from minor point. Corman created the films with other people's money, and with the prospect of distribution by other people, but he made them as an independent filmmaker. Contracts existed mostly on a film-by-film basis, and while supplying films for AIP Corman was also busy doing the same thing with Howco International, Allied Artists, United Artists, Twentieth Century-Fox and others. The films, for the most part, were made without the interference of a studio. It was Corman who, wearing the twin hats of producer and director in most cases, performed the roles of both creative artist and financial watchdog. Constraints on him, with few exceptions, were self-imposed.

The fact that he chose to work with low budgets implies that he desired the kind of freedom they offered, since as a low-budget, symbolically disenfranchised director, Corman could make "outlaw" films challenging the status quo (social or philosophical) without appearing overtly hypocritical. This facet of his work became much more visible after 1960, when Corman's work featured more socially conscious, often taboo subject matter including drugs, homosexuality, and race relations.

Corman's career indicates that creative expression can flourish under financial constraints, particularly for an artist as resolutely pessimistic as he was. While it may seem like freedom for a director not to have to worry about mismatched shots, or sets that look more like sets than like an illusion of reality, or actors that are not first, second, or even third choices for a role, a certain amount of deprivation also frees the director from the meddlesome presence of front-office bureaucrats, and takes him out of the conscious service of the culture at large, which uses film and other art forms to endorse its existence and its values. Other directors' careers support this idea. We think particularly of Edgar G. Ulmer, who made many great films not so much in spite of but surely because of the lack of large budgets and all that they imply. Ulmer's *Detour* as rendered by an MGM A-budget would have seemed ludicrous, and we can imagine Cedric Gibbons (no criticism of Gibbons) having a seizure on seeing the "set decoration" for the motel room in that film.

The same is true of Corman. He consciously chose to remain on low budgets, perhaps partly because of the need really to control and create, partly because of the "challenge" of making something significant without the means usually thought necessary, and, too, perhaps because he "set his sights low" and could not reconcile lavish budgets with his own self-image. Corman's forays into big-budget productions were sporadic, always preceded and followed by a return to the low-budgets he was more comfortable with.

During the mid to late 1950s, Corman put together a crew consisting most importantly of himself as producer/director, Floyd Crosby as photographer, Daniel Haller as art director, and a small stable of writers—Charles Griffith, Mark Hanna, Lou Rusoff, Richard Matheson, R. Wright Campbell, and Charles Beaumont. Part of Corman's fascination lies in his ability to convince artists like Crosby, Griffith, and Haller to work with him when major studio options would have been open to them. The reason for this would seem to be a combination of Corman's personal charisma and the fact that Haller and Crosby were also individualistic talents unable to work as cogs in the major studio bureaucratic machine. Corman's films displayed the talents of all three—we think of Crosby's swirling camera movements, Griffith's inspired mix-

ture of humor and horror, and Haller's exquisite rotting landscapes for
the Poe films—to spectacular advantage, in spite of his overall control
of the films.

Corman used companies like AIP and Allied to finance and distribute his films. In addition, he often visited film exchanges across the
country, where he could obtain financing and discuss with theater owners and distributors what ideas they thought could be successfully
translated into films. *Swamp Women* and *Teenage Doll* evolved out of
meetings with the Woolner Brothers in New Orleans.

Corman has commented frequently on having pow-wows with James
Nicholson and Samuel Arkoff at lunches at AIP. Films like *The Day the
World Ended* and *Attack of the Crab Monsters* were born in such in-
formal circumstances, with the three men discussing an idea, then
Corman taking it to one of his writers to develop a script. Corman has
said that during the 1970s he worked most closely with his New World
writer-directors on the story line and the editing, leaving the actual
shooting style to the director. The same was true during his long relationship with AIP and Allied, where he did his most significant work.
There were no studio hacks wandering over his sets, timing his shots,
or worrying about budget overruns. Corman did the worrying himself.

Because he controlled the films—being only subject to marketplace
considerations and budget limitations, again, self-imposed—Corman
bears the responsibility for his early successes and failures. Occasionally the distributors tampered with a film—*Carnival Rock* (1957) was
one example—but for the most part the films are intact, as he shot
them.

When Corman laughingly talks about making the early films in less
than ten days (a schedule Bill Warren said was "somewhat long for
Corman"!),[1] he is expressing pride at creating "something out of nothing," however trivial the "something" might be.

Breakneck filming schedules (we think of *Little Shop of Horrors*'s
two days and three nights) and minuscule budgets characterize Corman's entire career. Even his later, bigger budget productions like *The
St. Valentine's Day Massacre* or the Poe films have a plush look that
belies their actual cost.

Screenwriter-director Robert Towne, who wrote two of Corman's
films, has commented on the speed with which Corman shot most of
his films. Citing this speed as Corman's "downfall," Towne suggests
that Corman had a tendency to "measure things in the way he knew
best . . . with numbers" and "he felt that if he didn't do it quick he
did it wrong."[2] We can extend Towne's comments to see too much
emphasis on speed, or the preference for motion over stillness or con-
templation, as an avoidance mechanism, a desire to escape the "burden of identity." When an issue is dealt with quickly, it implies that

the issue may be too disturbing to dwell on. This brings us into areas of existential questioning that mirror those of the characters in Corman's films. A fast shooting schedule represents something more intense, more severe than a slow one, not only the desire to create something, but to create it quickly, to get it over with, as if the questions that creativity (acting, existing) raise are upsetting. Corman's pride at doing something with superhuman speed becomes relief at finishing it.

Low-Budget Aesthetics

To understand Corman's aesthetic, we must first understand that, more than any other single element, the fact of the low budget is responsible for the look and meaning of Corman's films.

Traditionally low-budget films—known earlier as "B" films—were created as a means of utilizing already-standing sets and already-contracted actors and other movie personnel to make a cheap film that would serve as a sort of warm-up for the major studio film it preceded. The "B" showed its second-class standing in its brief shooting schedule that resulted in rushed, ragged performances, sometimes startling continuity gaps, steadfast adherence to genre subjects with easily exploitable conventions, and, of course, sets that might tax audience credulity.

The low-budget film might have remained merely a pathetic reflection of its more expensive and "believable" counterpart, the "A," had not certain artists of great ability found themselves working in its confines. As is so often the case, the raw material of art—the sets, the actors, script, camera—could be transformed into something meaningful through the orchestrations of an artist: in this case, the director. According to convention, great art can emerge from poverty; we are all familiar with the "starving artist" of popular mythology. Much as we are tempted to dismiss this notion as a fantasy of the guilt-ridden haute bourgeoisie (also known as the corporate-academic establishment), the idea does hold significance for Corman.

Asked about the "utter bleakness" of his films, Corman replied that "you reflect what you see around you." We can extend this simple statement to say that the artist refashions the world as either an ideal image or a "real" one, that is, as he sees and experiences it. Corman's films "reflect what he sees," that is, they abound with failures, characters who react to the lack of meaning in life either by attempting to dismantle society (the gangster films, *Teenage Doll*) or by withdrawing into a fatally artificial, self-created world controlled by an unstable personality and in constant danger of collapse (the Poe films). Sometimes their lives are obsessed with the quest for meaning, expressed in characters of both great intelligence (Prince Prospero in *Masque of the Red Death*) and pathetic inarticulateness (Walter Paisley in *Bucket of Blood*). Whether this search is cast in the form of religious parable (*X— The Man with the X-Ray Eyes*), topical satire (*Bucket of Blood*), or Krameresque nuclear problem picture (*The Last Woman on Earth*), it nearly always masks the quest for identity, for personality integration, enlightenment. And what better way to express the repression of the ego, the hopelessness of this quest, than in characters who are themselves surrounded by a lack of "advantage," of the plush trappings we associate with the "idealized" world of movies, of an integrated, believable environment? Low-budget films cannot help but point out the dichotomy between the world of the film (two-dimensionality symbolizing the repression of the ego) and the "real" world outside the film (three-dimensionality, the illusion of it, symbolizing the emergence of ego, the attainment of the self). This dichotomy gives internal expression to the struggle of the characters, who exist in the flat, black and white, "unbelievable" world of *Teenage Doll* or *Attack of the Crab Monsters*, or the lush, artificial color world of the Poe films. The limits of the low-budget world of the films become the limits of the characters' world, an expression of their inability to move beyond, to break through the flatness, the artificiality around them. Even films that have an apparent social consciousness (*Teenage Doll, The Last Woman on Earth, The Wild Angels*) use their "message" to cover the philosophical quest that obsesses the characters. As David Will said, "There is no better medium than a cheap A.I.P. movie in which to convey such a cheap, rotten universe."[3]

One of the formal elements that figures strongly in this "low budget aesthetic" is the acting in Corman's films. Often criticized for the wildly varying styles evident in the films, Corman's use of actors is among the most detached of any director. John Alonzo has said he was surprised to see how "shy" Corman seemed in relation to the sex scenes in *Bloody Mama*, but Corman maintained a general "hands off" attitude toward the actors. For some actors, this is an ideal situation; they can create a characterization "in a void" that may be noticed because it differs from those around it, or because it works against the tone of the film. For an actor like Boris Karloff in *The Raven* this was a real problem, because Corman told him that the visuals were "covered," and that since Boris was the actor, he should *act*. Peter Bogdanovich commented once that Corman seemed intimidated by actors.

In terms of the kind of world Corman is presenting in the films, his approach makes sense. While Corman is in the godlike position of film creator, making a world, "directing" people (in a sense, creating and dominating them), he is also dealing with characters whose motive force is either the struggle for identity or a violent attack based on the recognized inability to achieve identity. In spite of the director's god-like position with respect to the film and its players, he knows he is not God, and withdraws from overt manipulation of his actors. This provides another paradigm for the quest for meaning, with Corman enacting the artist whose canvas is the set, but who, like the missing, modern God, refuses to get involved with humankind, to "direct their moves" or provide them with any answers. As in real life, the "actors" are left to find their own answers.

The Claustrophobic Frame

Corman's characters live in a bleak, often hopeless world surrounded by collapsing social institutions and death. There is no such thing as a "happy family" in any of his films. Indeed, families per se are extremely rare. While 1950s directors like Douglas Sirk and Nicholas Ray attacked the idea of a bourgeois entity such as the family, Corman went further by postulating a world in which families do not even exist. Typically his films show us a group of unrelated people thrown together either by the need for destruction and resurrection masquerading as "fate" (nuclear destruction in *The Day the World Ended*), or by distinctly antifamily, antisocial design (the youth gangs in *Teenage Doll*). Where a family does exist, it breaks family rules. In *Bloody Mama*, for example, the family is bound by such apparently negative values as robbery, murder, and incest.

In the early black-and-white films the world is characterized by a certain flatness, a lack of detailed furnishings that derives from budget limitations and indicates the paucity of opportunities available to the characters. The drab minimal sets of *The Day the World Ended*, *It Conquered the World*, and *The Undead* prominently illustrate this characteristic.

The locations in these films vary between extremely standardized houses and offices which rival Hugo Haas's interiors for sheer emptiness; and exteriors—forests, underpopulated city streets—which are hardly exploited for their vitality. The very dreariness of these black-and-white dramas is an early indication of Corman's view of the world as a closed, empty, pointless place.

This sense of hopelessness is reinforced by another typical low-budget ploy: the use of a limited number of actors. Like the calculated drabness of his early films, this focusing in on only a few people has obvious budgetary ramifications: fewer actors require less money. It was not uncommon for an actor in one of Corman's films to play two or more parts. In *Teenage Doll*, Ed Nelson appears first as a blind beggar, threatening the "doll" of the title. Later we see him well-scrubbed in a policeman's uniform. Beech Dickerson is probably the only actor in history to "play a tom-tom at my own funeral" after portraying both the dead man and a mourner in *Teenage Caveman*. (In a triumph of multilevel casting, he was also the bear that killed the dead man in this film.) Sometimes this "doubling" took place on both sides of the camera: in the 1960 triangle drama, *The Last Woman on Earth*, screenwriter Robert Towne also acted the role of the second lead under the pseudonym Ed Wain.

It would be misleading, however, to assume that Corman focused on small groups of people solely for reasons of budget. When the budgets increased, as in the Poe films, there is still a concentration on only a few characters, indicating Corman's basic feeling that the individual lives—and suffers—alone. *House of Usher*, for example, has only four principal actors. Occasionally this concentration on a handful of characters proved fatal, as in *Atlas*, a spectacle whose failure can be traced in part to its tiny group of actors.

The choice of natural locations in films like *Five Guns West* and *Apache Woman* fulfilled genre considerations (how many westerns could be shot indoors?), and allowed Corman to make the films cheaply. However, the outdoor films—with rare exceptions like *Bloody Mama*—gave him less control than the studio settings he favored, not to mention the incompatibility of open, outdoor, natural settings with Corman's closed, claustrophobic, and artificial viewpoint.

In a film like *Teenage Doll*, Corman's use of natural locations (city streets) is mitigated by the fact that the film is shot entirely at night, thus taking it out of the realm of "openness" suggested by outdoor locations and into the realm of psychological drama. Corman's rendering of the title character's no-exit situation is fleshed out by the use of *noir* elements, the most spectacular perhaps being Floyd Crosby's extreme high-angle shots of the girl running through a dark, depressing industrial landscape.

Widescreen Aesthetics

Another way in which Corman deemphasizes nature and shows both the film as an artificial construct and the hopelessness these characters experience isolated from nature is by stretching the image with various widescreen formats (mostly Panavision). As is typical with Corman, we see aesthetic qualities deriving from practical considerations. A surprising number of late 1950s and early 1960s low budget films were shot in widescreen, and this includes black and white (Superscope for *Machine Gun Kelly*) and color (*Five Guns West*, Corman's first directorial effort). Though it took low-budget filmmakers longer than the majors to utilize Cinemascope after Fox popularized it in 1953, they used it far more than might have been expected. 'Scope was a reasonably inexpensive way of "opening up" a picture, of making it literally and figuratively bigger than normal. The phrase "widescreen" also proved advantageous in marketing a low-budget film.

Corman has disavowed any aesthetic purpose behind his use of 'scope, but among directors perhaps only Preminger and Minnelli have embraced it as thoroughly. The fact is that Corman shot about half of his films in widescreen, long after the novelty of the form had worn off and many considered it frivolous or difficult to work with. During a brief sojourn at Columbia Studios in the 1960s, Corman learned that a film he was making there was being shot flat in spite of his understanding (and wish) that it be shot widescreen. The ensuing altercation between Corman and the cameraman, then Corman and Columbia, resulted in Corman quitting and receiving a contract settlement from the studio.

What does 'scope really imply? Primarily it calls attention to itself, to the film as a closed artistic construct, a patently false, unreal world in which even the dimensions of the space the characters inhabit are controlled. Artifice is indicated rather than disguised, and the entrapment of Corman's characters (using a device that ironically is intended to "expand" the film!) in a false, closed world over which they have no control is validated. Corman's expertise with 'scope is shown particularly in the Poe films, where he developed foreground/background tension in his imagery, and created, for films like *House of Usher*, resonant montage sequences of the idealized world of the past.

Color as Style

Another way for Corman to "open up" the films—to have them taken seriously by public and press—was in his use of color. His first film, in 1955, was color, at a time when many major studio films were still being shot in black-and-white. In the early days, until 1962 with *Tower of London*, his last black-and-white film, Corman alternated between color and black-and-white, with all the early science fiction and horror films in black-and-white, and the "outdoor films" like *Swamp Women* or *Thunder over Hawaii* (among his least successful efforts) shot in color.

In 1960, with *House of Usher*, Corman's use of color became a stylistic hallmark instead of merely an economically justified means of increasing his audience. There was a sense of conscious exploitation of color to reflect mood and distressed psychological states. This heightened attention to color came about probably because Corman had longer shooting schedules, bigger budgets, and controlled studio settings, and because he worked closely on color schemes and furnishings with Daniel Haller, who had been with him since *War of the Satellites* in 1958.

The sense of flatness and drabness remarked in many of the early films (and visible even as late as 1960 in the color film *The Last Woman on Earth*) is not present in *House of Usher*. If anything, *Usher* and the films that follow it create a world dense and overripe to the point of rottenness. Corman fills his frames with images of rot and decay that signify his obsession (through death-obsessed lead characters) with death. He still used a limited number of actors, so the films retain a slightly "behavioral" slant, even though the characters sometimes appear dwarfed by Haller's rich, rather massive sets.

If we can generalize for the sake of argument to say that black and white (which are *not* the colors of the real world) signifies the entrapment of the ego, and by extension, death (the ultimate repression of the ego), then color would seem to indicate the opposite. If black and white, being an absence of color, of life and vitality, indicates a leveling or breakdown of ego, then color would seem to offer at least the possibility of ego emergence, since color represents both "life" and "the world" as we know it. The Poe films bear this out on a surface level. With their overrich decor and vivid color schemes, they indicate a feeling of life. Yet this is undercut both by the characters who populate the strikingly colored environments of *Masque of the Red Death* and *The Pit and the Pendulum*, and by the images Corman calls into play to express his bleak attitudes.

Conformity and Identity

Who are these characters? In the important early films such as *It Conquered the World* or *Teenage Caveman*, the central character is a scientist or other "truthseeker" obsessed with finding answers to the philosophical questions that plague mankind. Even in a throwaway effort like *Viking Women and the Sea Serpent*, the central characters embark on a search with mythic overtones.

Corman's films show man as a passive, servile, conforming creature, victimized by natural forces only the lead "truthseeker" or the supersensitive aesthete seems to be aware of. He seeks to find some way to violate the natural order of things. As H. P. Lovecraft said, "Time, space, and natural law hold for me suggestions of intolerable bondage, and I can form no picture of emotional satisfaction which does not involve their defeat. . . ."[4] These "natural forces" are seen not as healthy, liberating forces but as mysterious traps that hold mankind back.'

Corman's characters, at least those who have not given up entirely, inevitably drop out of conformist society in order to "discover" some secret that will offer hope and meaning for their lives. A "grass is greener" posture is struck, wherein it is imagined that something better exists "beyond the vortex" (*Viking Women and the Sea Serpent*),

"beyond the river" (*Teenage Caveman*), or in the past (*The Undead*).
In *It Conquered the World,* scientist Tom Anderson allows for the invasion of earth by aliens he thinks will make a better world, when,
instead, they plan to enslave it. In nearly every case, the search for
truth, enlightenment, or self-actualization ends with the destruction of
the one who "dared" to step out of line, to risk the backlash of malevolent natural forces. The only relief is found in nonidentity, in dissolving the individual into the group, which is virtually identical to the
process of seeking truth and being destroyed for it. In both cases, identity remains elusive.

Artifice and Nature

Corman shows the paradox of the two worlds of existence—the material present that entraps, and the spiritual "other," a psychic zone
that offers the hope of liberation through an integration of the tormented human personality with the spiritual "other." Frequently this
"other" is merely the protagonist's seductive memories of the past
(*House of Usher*), or the "lost" memory of the prenuclear past, where,
culture having been gutted, a new civilization begins to emerge that
involves conflict between the remnants of the past and present (*The
Day the World Ended*). The interplay between natural and studio locations in films like *It Conquered the World* and *The Undead* points
up this dichotomy.

By the time of *Teenage Doll* in 1957, even the hope for liberation
has begun to disappear, indicated here by the preponderance of interiors and a rendering even of natural, outdoor settings as utterly
claustrophobic through the use of extreme high-angle shots, night photography, and an integration that might be termed a "swallowing up"
of character by landscape.

A Bucket of Blood and *The Little Shop of Horrors* continue the
trend toward internalization, with most of their scenes occurring either
in the apartment of the nebbish-hero or at his hostile place of employment. *Little Shop of Horrors* continues *Teenage Doll's* approach to natural locations by showing the typical city street as a slum environment
populated by winos and vagrants.

With *House of Usher,* Corman went formally and entirely "indoors."
Always somewhat bothered by the uncontrollable aspects of location
shooting, with the irritating presence of "natural" sounds and events
always potentially conflicting with the film, Corman dispensed almost
entirely with the real world in favor of one fabricated completely from
studio sets. Ironically, one of the most famous shots in the Poe films,
one repeated from film to film, is the severe low-angle matte shot of
the castle in which the tormented protagonist lives. This is theoreti-

cally an "outdoor" shot, that is, a representation of the world outside the castle. In actuality it is as artificial as the world outside, since it is not even a real building but a painting of one, with the image conjoining the clearly two-dimensional castle with a shot of a real sea cliff below which crash huge waves. This shot is repeated usually two or three times during the course of the drama, but it is primarily a false rendering of the real world, a false reminder that such a world exists. This makes sense in terms of the internalized world of the films, a world at whose center stands a self-obsessed, godlike but utterly passive character, Nicholas Medina or Roderick Usher. For such men there is no real world, no world outside their carefully contrived environment, fancifully, plushly furnished with evidence of their past, their tradition, the whole stream of their history, which allows them to suspend detested natural laws and pretend that death does not exist.

A Unifying Theme

If the films could be said to have an overriding theme, it would have to be the intrusive, overwhelming fear of death, the absurdity of human existence in light of this most "natural" phenomenon. This ties together other strands in the Corman oeuvre, including the attempt to establish the self, and the revulsion at sexuality noted particularly in the Poe films.

In *Teenage Doll*, the central image is the dead body of Nan Baker, which Corman brutally introduces when a dishwasher unwittingly throws a pan of dirty dishwater on her body lying in the predawn street. Corman returns to this image several times in the film, and it is the catalyst for everything that happens in the film. In *Machine Gun Kelly,* the title character plays against genre expectations by portraying the murderous but petty gangster as a death-obsessed coward, paralyzed by fear when he sees a skull tattoo or a coffin being carried into a building.

In many of the films the setting is the world after the wholesale destruction of humanity, as opposed to individual death. *The Day the World Ended, Teenage Caveman*, and *The Last Woman on Earth* take place after all but a handful of people have been destroyed.

The Poe films are based entirely on death-obsessed characters, but there is the added dimension of a sexuality somehow perverse (*House of Usher*), unsatisfying (*Tomb of Ligeia*), or impotent (*The Pit and the Pendulum*). Corman fills these films with symbols of death. We think of the image of Elizabeth Medina trapped in the Iron Maiden, a kind of upright coffin; of the preponderance of actual coffins, a double image of the body, with the prematurely buried body inside a symbol of man's soul, his torment; of the violent visualizations of the title objects from

The Pit and the Pendulum; of the destruction of personality by an attack on the eyes (*Tomb of Ligeia*).

Corman fleshes out this despairing world with a combination of montage and long takes highlighted by camerawork of extreme mobility. The sense of "aliveness" we have from films like *The Pit and the Pendulum* or *Masque of the Red Death* could hardly come from the inert, psychologically dead characters at their center. Corman creates a feeling of tension and dynamics by incorporating moving camera (Francesca's vain flight through the castle in *Masque of the Red Death*), dialectical montage (the staccato intercutting between the pendulum, its operator, and its victim in *The Pit and the Pendulum*), and formal montage sequences incorporating laboratory opticals (the breathtaking montage of the verdant past in *House of Usher*).

Summary

Corman should be seen primarily as a modernist filmmaker, employing extremely standardized Hollywood genres (gangsters, science fiction, horror) and creating new ones (black comedy, juvenile delinquency) to articulate a violently antiromantic, existential view of life. Like other directors during the pivotal postwar decade of the 1950s, Corman devoted equal attention to exploring and annihilating the very idea of genre, for example, making four homogenized westerns that superficially support that genre's concern with the struggle between nature and civilization, while undermining the generic structure of those films by casting women rather than men in all the major roles. If genre exists fundamentally to validate the values of the culture out of which it arises (a "culture" comprised not only of the "real life" of America but the traditions of the film studios in general and low-budget filmmakers in particular), Corman's use of genre is simultaneously supportive and destructive of culture.

The films bear out this concept in other ways. Most of Corman's own directorial efforts (and we must distinguish between the films he created and those he produced for others) portray two societies in violent opposition to each other. The first is the "real world"—the somewhat dull, anonymous world of conformity and mass behavior, embodied, for example, in the townspeople of *It Conquered the World* or the nurse/doctor/policeman in *Not of This Earth*. Corman contrasts this world with the excessively stylized environments created by a—usually male—scientific or mystic-aesthetic personality as a more favorable alternative. This is a world characterized by individual rather than mass psychology, by a feeling of "otherness" sometimes marked by a dislocation in time (*The Undead*), but more often by an overall—and temporary—suspension of the hated laws of nature and reality (*Bucket of Blood*, the Poe films). The self-created world-within-a-world can exist only as long as its inventor, and Corman shows its literal destruction by ritual purgation (fire in *The House of Usher* and *The Tomb of Ligeia*, water in *The Terror*) at the point of the collapse of the personality that created it. The "hated laws" that cause the invention of an alternate world are usually personality problems, including social maladjustment (*Bucket of Blood*), obsession with enlightenment (*It Conquered the World*), and sexual impotence (*The Pit and the Pendulum*), but the most important hated law, the most important reality in life for Corman's characters (and the one they try most strongly to overcome), is death.

If we could select two images that most strongly typify Corman's worldview, we might choose for the first the destruction of a brilliant but weak male by a powerfully sexual female in a crumbling edifice. (In a fundamental reversal of Poe, Corman's films completely de-intellectualize the female to make the male/female personality a combination of impotent male artist and active female anima.) This occurs not only in the Poe films, but in many of Corman's seemingly "straight" genre pictures including *The Gunslinger* and *Machine Gun Kelly*. In the Poe films, this scene, which usually climaxes the film, portrays the encounter as the final, bloody embrace between two characters who have attempted to destroy each other throughout the film: the male, a supersensitive but impotent aesthete who re-creates the "ugly reality" of a sexually demanding female as an untouchable creature (she is apparently dead, yet "lives on" in beloved representations in the form of a preserved corpse or a painting by the male); the female, a terrifying embodiment of unsatisfied impulses who "survives death" (in *The House of Usher* she breaks out of the coffin to strangle her brother) to wreak havoc on the male and bring about the literal destruction of his world.

Our second typical Corman image—one that, again, constantly recurs—is the attempted "rescue" of a supposedly dead being from the bondage of the grave. This image, which derives from Poe, is familiar in the Poe series, where it is usually the event that triggers the destruction of the fragile world of the film, but we see it also in examples of such seemingly antithetical, nonfantastic genres as the war film (*The Secret Invasion*). This attack on a coffin or a prison to free a trapped being is a flawless metaphor for the attempt by an individual to resolve the mind-body conflict by setting free the mind/soul/spirit from the bondage of a body, which must decay and die. In one of the earliest such attacks in Corman's work—in *The Pit and the Pendulum*—the collapse of an already teetering personality (Nicholas Medina) quickly follows this doomed project.

In both these images, Corman portrays a divided consciousness, neither male nor female identity complete in itself, longing for self-actualization but ultimately self-destroying. The dynamics of most of his films are nihilistic rather than life-affirming, with an overall movement away from coherency and totality toward division and chaos.

This derives largely from Corman's concern with the problem—the impossibility—of satisfactory human existence in light of the fact of death. Most of his films deal with this incontrovertible ending to life, not only the Poe films where it is fairly obvious, but in the early thrillers such as *The Day the World Ended* or *Teenage Doll*. The fear of death is not only in the cessation of personality, but in the even more frightening possibility that death offers only a false hope of peace, the idea that even death is somehow "not real" but merely a more hopeless, more immobilizing version of the entrapment, dissatisfaction, paralysis that, for Corman, constitutes life—Guy Carrell's dilemma in *The Premature Burial*.

Corman's world view not only excludes any possible optimism (with rare exceptions such as *Teenage Caveman* or *Gas-s-s-s*), but it specifically employs the concept of "seeing"—understanding, enlightenment—as merely another, perhaps the most significant, avenue toward self-destruction. Dr. Xavier's experiments with sight in *X—The Man with the X-Ray Eyes* increase his sense of paranoia and horror as he sees through everything, to its "true nature." The essence of life is sordid, pitiless, hopeless—it does not bear viewing. Many of the director's important characters are exceptionally "attuned": mentally advanced, with supersensitive sight or hearing or other senses (Roderick Usher in *The House of Usher*, Verden Fell in *The Tomb of Ligeia*), and this increased understanding takes them out of the undifferentiated mass of humanity. But they are destroyed for their understanding. The liberal-humanist cliché that "Knowledge is power" is entirely reversed in Corman's films—the more his characters learn and "see," the more passive, alienated, and self-destructive they are. The number of suicides in his films is significant, from Walter Paisley covering himself in clay and hanging himself in *Bucket of Blood* to Herman Barker turning his shotgun on his own face in *Bloody Mama*.

2

The World Destroyed

THE MOST SIGNIFICANT EVENT in modern times—the nuclear devastation of Hiroshima and Nagasaki and the resulting widespread awakening to the possibility of human self-annihilation—has been widely portrayed in both fantastic and realistic film genres. Few filmmakers have dealt directly with this phenomenon more than once, and the most famous postnuclear war dramas are not typical of their creators' careers: for example, Arch Oboler's *Five*, Stanley Kramer's *On the Beach*, or Ranald MacDougall's *The World, the Flesh, and the Devil*. Often the "bomb film" shows more interest in the mechanics leading up to atomic destruction than in the bleak happenings that follow it: for example, Stanley Kubrick's *Dr. Strangelove* or Sidney Lumet's *Fail Safe*.

As was often the case when dealing with unpleasant, unsettling events, the low-budget studios attacked this theme with far greater relish than the majors, often using radioactivity as an excuse for presenting mutated monsters, from the giant crabs of Corman's *Attack of the Crab Monsters* to the oversize humans of Bert I. Gordon's *War of the Colossal Beast*. Even where radioactivity is not directly blamed for these mutations, as in Nathan Juran's *Attack of the 50-Foot Woman*, the bleak settings—most frequently the desert—show an atmosphere of postnuclear destruction in which nature itself becomes violently, murderously unpredictable.

While many 1950s monster films dealt with the effects of radioactivity on a previously harmonious and balanced nature, few went so far as to show a world completely destroyed. Roger Corman probably directed more feature films that begin *after* the bomb than any other filmmaker, and a hindsight overview of his career suggests how well this approach reflects Corman's general attitude. Most of his films show a self-contained world, fragile and precarious, invented by a dissatisfied, unactualized personality as an alternative to the hopeless real world. This includes not only the Poe films, but science fiction (*The Day the World Ended*), gangster films (*Bloody Mama*), even black

The merging of active monster and passive human in The Day the World Ended.   19

comedy (*Bucket of Blood*). Corman's view of the world as a place of either utter hopelessness or malevolent destruction of individual identity (evidenced most strongly in the horrifying things Dr. Xavier "sees" when he expands his "vision" in *X—Man with the X-Ray Eyes*) implies a need for wholesale destruction which is accomplished by a ritual purgation by fire (*House of Usher*) or water (*The Terror*), or simply by a destruction of the individual(s) whose world the film encompasses (*It Conquered the World, Bloody Mama*). World collapse is implied in individual self-destruction.

Conversely, Corman uses nuclear destruction as a metaphor for the collapse of individual consciousness. Typically, he isolates a few individuals in a hopeless, hostile environment (*The Day the World Ended, Attack of the Crab Monsters*), detailing their methodical destruction in the face of social chaos, their inability to deal with life stripped of buttressing social institutions and "order." Even in a film like *Not of This Earth*, which follows more in the tradition of overcivilized aesthetes from *It Conquered the World, The Undead*, and the Poe films, nuclear destruction is the background motive for the arrival on Earth of the agent for Earth's destruction.

According to Paul Willeman, the director's preoccupation with the world's destruction expresses "the wish to transcend life in order to return to paradise, motivated by the memory of the Golden Age. . . ."[1] Because this desire cannot always be consciously articulated (since it posits the absolutely unacceptable idea that modern life is intolerable and *must* be escaped), this "movement toward paradise" is often visualized as a threatened destruction, for example, a takeover of Earth by superior aliens. It is most significant that Corman rarely fleshes out the image of "paradise," but uses it only as a device, the distant goal, that may be achieved through the leveling of Earth and the individuals who inhabit it.

The Day the World Ended

Corman shot *The Day the World Ended* (1955), according to producer Alex Gordon, on "a tight 10-day schedule,"[2] for $96,000. Most of the action occurs in and around a secluded, typical 1950s California ranch house, protected from the mass destruction of nuclear war by a preponderance of natural, shielding lead in the hills around it. The house is owned by retired navy captain Jim Maddison, who has spent years preparing a safe environment for the anticipated "T. D. Day" ("Total Destruction"), only to find it invaded by a handful of other survivors who arrive there by accident. Superficially the film seems to resemble a typical genre effort showing the evolving relationships in a group forced into close communion. But *The Day the World Ended* goes far beyond its problem picture origins to show what Jerry Kutner has called a world of "pure archetype."[3]

Corman posits a clear antagonism between God and mankind in the opening montage that shows the collapse of civilization during "T. D. Day." A booming overdub quotes biblical verses as an image of the rolling heavens gives way to shots of mass destruction, from the epic— the dreaded mushroom cloud, enormous buildings reduced to shells— to the intimate—a fetid pool through which fish swim. This is an alienated view of God, commenting on the dead earth that He created. Corman counters this cold image with a series of graceful dissolves that follow the credits, showing the arrival of five more characters into the house now occupied by two. The postwar ambience is one of billowing smoke, through which these characters stumble. The impermanence of the environment (which recalls those in the openings of several of Edgar G. Ulmer's films, most notably *Strange Illusion* and *Detour*) changes as Corman switches from outside the house to the inside, where the images are sharp. Thus the characters travel from exteriors that have "no fixity," to use John Belton's phrase, to the at least hopeful reality of the house.

Corman introduces one of his most fascinating characters in these early dissolves, the well-named Radek (Paul Dubov). In a career filled with films that show two kinds of worlds—the unsatisfying "real" and the "artificial," wish-fulfillment alternative—it is not surprising to find a plethora of characters who travel between the two, who seem to exist in both. Radek is the ultimate expression of this type: a human being who survives the blast, but with a half-human and half-mutated face, with spidery white burns running down the side. Corman's camera follows Radek as he stumbles through the fog, resting the camera at ground level as he falls, apparently dead. But he is not dead. His first words on being discovered by another character (and, significantly, the first words any character speaks in the film), the geologist Rick (Richard Denning), are simple ones: "Kill me." Rick chooses not to do this, and risks his and every one else's lives by not only refusing to kill Radek, but bringing him into the house and risking contamination.

Jim Maddison had hoped to survive with only his daughter Louise (Lori Nelson), but the arrival of the others forces him to rethink his strategies. In the absence of a compassionate God, Maddison assumes the role, taking complete control of the group. His rule is based on an increasingly more epic view of his own power, which takes him so far as to tell Rick that the latter can shoot Louise, his own daughter, "if you have to," that is, if she becomes contaminated by one of the "monsters" roaming around in the hills outside. The film contrasts him with Rick. Whereas Maddison wants to destroy Radek, thinking only of the group's immediate safety, Rick argues that they must allow Radek to live, as it becomes obvious that Radek spends more of his time among the monsters, and may hold some kind of key to a solution of their problems.

Corman teases the audience with only occasional glimpses of Radek's "world," which is now the real world outside the safety of the house, until late in the film. Certainly these two spheres are heavily contrasted throughout, with Maddison's godlike, regimented control of food and "the water in the sealed jars" being the hallmark of the world of the last uncontaminated humans, and the briefly seen trapping and killing of a rabbit, along with vague, fog-drenched shots of a mysterious "monster" the images of Radek's world.

Corman uses so many dissolves in this film that they become a thematic element, the presence of the threatening exterior world constantly fading in and out of the interior world. This theme is made more concrete by the script's treatment of Louise as an unwilling conduit between them. Like Radek she moves between the two worlds. Her conversation is much bleaker than her father's; being "blunt by nature," he asks her if she likes Rick, then immediately, "Could you love him?" She initially refuses to hear of mating with Rick in order to preserve the race, believing "there is to be no future." Several shots of her looking at a picture of herself with her fiancé taken during the halcyon days before nuclear destruction show her depressed state. This feeling leaves her open to telepathic communication from her now completely mutated fiancé, who wanders through the hills outside in a state of evolving adaptation. Several times she "hears something" that others nearby (usually Rick) cannot hear. Eventually contact is made as the "monster" lures her into the woods and tries to make contact, though it is clear from the way it acts that no harm is intended.

Each time one of the characters—none of them adapted to their new environment—enters the "real world," they risk contamination. Radek alone is able to come and go unscathed. His earlier pleading with Rick to "kill me" becomes "I'm not going to die . . . I thought I was, but I'm not." From this point on, Radek begins to disappear for long periods, returning only to rest, because "I have an enemy who wants to kill me." The character becomes more fascinating as his personality undergoes changes. He becomes a "pawn of evolution" as Rick theorizes that radioactivity has speeded up evolutionary change to a breakneck pace. Radek understands what is happening to him, beyond any logical credibility; he realizes he needs red meat rather than what the others are eating in order to support his adaptation to a nuclear environment. His success "out there" becomes apparent in his sinister, mocking amusement at the others, as well as his secret knowledge: "I'm not afraid . . . I like it out there. . . . There are wonderful things going on out there . . . some time I'll tell you . . . you're all going to die." The other characters are literally powerless to touch him: aside from the threat of his radioactivity, they are afraid of him and the changes in human identity he may foreshadow in them.

The film contains a great deal of religious imagery of a decidedly downbeat nature. From the opening godlike narrator who describes the destruction rather than creation of the world, we pass to Rick, whose brother, we learn, was killed, even though he was preparing to be "a man of God." Characters make numerous references to the Bible, but particularly Maddison, from whom we expect this attitude. Mainly self-protective rather than truth-seeking like Rick, Maddison looks with some vague hope at the Bible, feeling it may offer a possibility of salvation. He chides the gangster Tony Lamont for entirely rejecting the Bible. Yet the film's final, basically optimistic ending depends on the reassertion of God, the cleansing of the valley specifically and the earth in general by God's rain, which, it is implied, purifies the air even as it destroys the monsters, the mutations who have no protection against it.

Mental telepathy is an early Corman/Griffith theme—and something of a breakthrough idea in 1950s science fiction, as Bill Warren has pointed out—that finds expression in *The Day the World Ended*. A major aspect of *Not of This Earth* and *Attack of the Crab Monsters*, where it is verbalized as an overdub that substitutes for speech, it exists in *The Day the World Ended* as an unspecific link between the two worlds that exist within the film. The "lure of monsters," of the terrifying world "outside" the regular, predictable world, is a powerfully felt force among Corman characters; here it is Louise who feels it, as her mutated fiancé uses telepathic communication to seduce her outside. (A year later Corman would show another character mesmerized by a monster using nonspeech communication in *It Conquered the World*.) Corman's fascination with these human monsters is strong, and the film makes clear in spite of genre-influenced horror effects (the shadow of the monster passing over her bedroom wall as she sleeps) that the monster is as much victim as villain. Part of the resonance of this concept derives from the faltering attempts of the "monster" to communicate with its human counterpart—the desire by the divided consciousness to reunite. These later scenes of Louise passing between the two worlds are foreshadowed not only by Radek, but by another half-mutated character who, dying, begs the others for food, imparting a brief horrific sketch of what is happening "out there" before he dies: "others . . . stronger than me, much stronger, not many but strong." Thus he makes concrete the vague threat the helpless little group feels in its enclosed environment. From this point their own paranoia increases, as Ruby harasses the others into looking at her skin "becoming hard."

The corruption of Maddison's world-within-a-world is also documented. The film sees the need to reassert the normal order of things, but it is unclear how this can come about with the group that is the focus of the story. Maddison's iron rule shows a character unopposed to duplicating the "mistakes" of God as he verbalizes his willingness to kill his daughter for a greater good. (He is also one of only two human characters in the story who kill; the other is the one *he* kills, Tony, whose opportunism makes him an easily despisable character, contrasted with Maddison, who alternates between benevolent patriarch and fascistic manipulator. Contrast this further with Rick, who fights both humans—Tony—and monster—the fiancé—but never kills.)

Most of the other characters show their need for destruction rather than redemption and survival. The gangster Tony treats his girl friend with maliciousness and eventually kills her, in a brutally frank scene in which he stabs her, says "Happy landing," and throws her from a cliff. The single throwaway character, never properly integrated into the story, is an old prospector who wanders around with his mule. He is clearly at his life's end, thus dismissing him from consideration as a survivor. Only Rick and Louise seem suitable to pass from the old world into the new, but according to the melodramatic model, Louise must confront her past—the mutated fiancé—before she is free to join Rick as the parents of the new race. Rick's suitability is immediately obvious; Louise's obsession with her fiancé and her past, and her articulated sense of hopelessness, stand in the way of self-realization. It is not accidental that the change in her personality is accompanied by the cleansing rain which ends the film. The reassertion of God in this case must accompany the self-realization of an individual in the insular world of Corman's films, just as the absence or malevolence of God triggers individual self-destruction.

Of course, the ending is not entirely optimistic. On the level of plot, we realize that Rick and Louise may be leaving one dead environment (the house, which has no more living inhabitants) for another (the blasted earth). On a formal level, Corman shows this by inserting a very rapid dissolve between shots of the departing, smiling couple, showing the image of the dead monster. This can be interpreted in two ways: as an indication that the threat the monster represented has evaporated; or as a suggestion that this creature will either be duplicated "out there" or will be carried strongly in the memory of Rick and Louise, thus preventing any true self-actualization.

Attack of the Crab Monsters

Corman recalls *Attack of the Crab Monsters* (1956), his first film for Allied Artists, as "*the* most successful of all the early low budget horror movies," a fact he attributes to the film's structure. During preparation of the project, he asked screenwriter Charles Griffith to plot the film as a series of cliffhanger scenes, an idea he extends to the very last shot in the film. Corman's further comments on this film reveal much about his attitudes toward filmmaking: "in horror and science fiction films, too much time is usually spent explaining the characters in depth and developing various subplots."[4] This apparently simple comment shows Corman's intentional subjugation of actors to atmosphere, a concept that underlies not only *Attack of the Crab Monsters* but most of his films. The "atmosphere" of *Attack of the Crab Monsters* is characterized by entrapment in nature (a small group of scientists is stranded on an island with no contact with the outside world) and hopelessness (they are being destroyed one by one by a group of giant crabs).

Corman opens the film with a typical "teaser" segment quoted verbatim from later in the film. Martha Hunter (Pamela Duncan) awakes in bed to a disembodied voice coaxing her to "come outside" and "help me." She follows the voice through rough terrain, and stops at the edge of a huge pit. The earth begins to shake, and, the voice still leading her onward, she faints at the pit's rim. This mysterious scene not only entices the audience, it also sets the tone for the film that follows. Above all, *Attack of the Crab Monsters* is characterized by an air of utter mystery—its characters barely defined, the origins and purpose of the mutant crabs only hinted at, all centered in an island landscape that is literally disintegrating beneath their feet, into the sea.

Corman establishes the preeminence of the environment—the sea— in Floyd Crosby's resonant shots that follow the credit sequence (reminding us of Crosby's association with Murnau for *Tabu*). But the epic calm of the water is immediately broken by a series of mostly stock-footage shots of exploding atomic bombs that form the film's now obligatory (after *The Day the World Ended*) destruction-montage. The idea of nature-in-reverse and a Creator by turns indifferent and evil is validated by this montage, which combines a relentless string of atomic explosions, seen from many angles, with a cosmic overdub that says, "And the Lord said I will destroy man whom I have created from the face of the earth. . . ." As in *The Day the World Ended* and *Teenage Caveman* Corman uses a montage to render an ironic version of "Creation," with a godlike commentary accompanying images of mass annihilation.

The story concerns a group of scientists who arrive at an island in the Pacific to investigate the disappearance of a previous group of scientists who had been sent to examine "fallout effects at their worst," from a nearby "H Bomb test." The current group is composed of biologists, botanists, and nuclear physicists—in short, the same kind of group that came before them and disappeared. This initial "doubling"

The last survivors await death in Attack of the Crab Monsters.

of the group prepares us for the film's primary theme of the attempt by a divided consciousness to reunite its parts. The scientific aspects of their search make up much of the film's plot, with each person contributing his or her theory about "what is happening." But this scientific, practical, "real," and logical explanation is shown as an ironic counterpoint to the film's metaphysical concerns: the scientists' training and knowledge are utterly powerless against the same threat that destroyed their predecessors—a group of gigantic, mutant crabs with telepathic powers is simultaneously tunneling through the island, destroying it from within, and luring one by one each member of the scientific party into the "pit" and into a state of absorption "inside" the crabs.

The abnormal, suspended-from-reality nature of the island is immediately apparent to the arriving group. Dr. Karl Weigand (Leslie Bradley), the only member of the group to constantly wear dark glasses, says, "something in the air is wrong." Jules Devereaux (Mel Welles) mentions "the lack of welcome, lack of abiding life." Ensign Quinlan (Ed Nelson) explains it is because there is "no sound . . . no animal life of any kind," since the island appears to be devoid of animals except for seagulls, which come and go as they please, and land crabs, which live in two environments—the island and the sea. The threat of the new land is validated by the death, only moments after the film begins, of a seaman, whose head is cut off by "something" below the water's surface.

The film abounds with what appear to be obvious Freudian images. The beheading of the seaman, along with Jules Devereaux's hand being chopped off, can be seen as symbols of castration anxiety. This idea is furthered by the presence of the "pit," a huge hole "at least 50 feet deep" that develops shortly after the group's arrival, and an area into which the crabs lure the scientists to their deaths. The characters' gravitation at the end to a communication tower—a clear phallic symbol—could signal an attempt to reestablish the patriarchal status quo, the reuniting of the ego. But the film treats these events as more than Freudian symbolism—indeed, the island itself is rendered as a broad symbol of collapsing consciousness, with the idea of the split personality seeking its integrated state continuously validated both by the film's events and by its setting.

Three environments, or "worlds," exist within the film: the highest, most civilized level is the surface of the island, with the makeshift headquarters of the investigating party the only (but temporary, it seems) haven against the monsters. The second is the area below the island's surface but above the sea: the caves and tunnels and pits that characterize the island. These caves and tunnels multiply as the giant crabs burrow through them, slowly collapsing the island into the sea. The third world is that of the sea, the basest level from which the crabs are born and grow. The film details the attempts by creatures that live in the two lower levels to destroy the uppermost. It envisions these creatures as "monsters," significantly man-made mutations (the result of foolish experiments with nuclear weapons) mysteriously bent on the destruction of the pitiful group stranded on the island. When Hank Chapman (Russell Johnson) asks "why" the monsters should want to destroy the island by tunneling through it, Karl replies, almost matter-of-factly, "To get at us, of course." It is significant that Karl should say this, since the film links him most strongly with the crabs, and with an intelligence that most nearly understands what is happening.

The crabs "talk" to the group through a kind of telepathic articulation embodied in the voices of those it has "eaten." At first the monsters attempt to persuade the group to leave the relative safety of their cabin, by begging ("Help me," says McClain to Martha Hunter) or teasing ("Something remarkable has happened"), appealing to their humanity or their scientific curiosity. Eventually, they use their human victims as ironic mouthpieces for the destruction of the small party, expanding the horror of the group's dilemma by reminding it how powerless humanity is when compared to the crabs: "Will you grow new lives when I have taken yours from you?".

The film drops occasional red herrings to the audience, mostly centered on the character of Karl Weigand. He stands out from the group visually by the presence of dark glasses—an illogical symbol since none of the others wears them, but one that links him with the world of the destructive unconscious symbolized by the crabs. While the others seem completely mystified, Karl takes charge and leads them through some of the tunnels, appearing to have what one of the others refers to as a "small secret." He is the most bold in seeking out the crabs, but also the most sympathetic to them; when Dale Drewer (Richard Garland) refuses to enter the caves, Karl convinces him to proceed, saying, "They are like a rattlesnake" in making their proximity obvious. He tries to appeal to Martha's scientific orientation by saying, rather than kill them, "Wouldn't you like to examine a live specimen?"—hardly a possibility given the creatures' size and ruthless attempts to destroy them all.

The film's linking of Karl to the crabs, however, seems merely a diversion from the core of the film, a device, as in whodunits, to compound the air of mystery. Similarly, *Attack of the Crab Monsters almost* sets up a romantic triangle between Martha, Dale, and Hank. Again, this leads nowhere, as Corman shows no interest in developing "characters in depth," a strategy that makes absolute sense in a film that deals with lost characters seeking enlightenment.

As in *The Day the World Ended* and *It Conquered the World*, two films in the same genre, characters feel the "lure of the other," a spiritual world outside the norm that, while clearly fraught with danger, also offers the possibility of personality integration and purpose. The world around them is quickly disappearing. Martha looks out to the sea from the cabin and says, "Once upon a time there was a mountain. . . ." Asked to explain, she says that the day before there was a mountain rising out of the sea, clearly visible. "Now it's gone." The regularity and harmony of nature has been destroyed, and it is only a matter of time before the entire island, as one of the crabs tells them, "vanishes beneath the waves of the sea." The crabs, when not busy destroying the island, play on the characters' need for meaning and integration, by luring them into the "pit," where the previous group is believed to be. When they leave the safety of the cabin, they are destroyed. What appears to be a possible discovery of the "missing self" symbolized by the missing earlier party is actually the total collapse of personality, the yielding of the conscious—represented by the human characters safe in their cabin on the island's highest ground—to the unconscious—represented by the malignant crabs, by the absorption of the human personality into the "other" of lost identity.

The crabs verbalize a plan to destroy all of mankind after this initial group is killed and their island, their world, is buried in the sea. At this point they become linked with a Creator who destroys, a force outside the human group controlling its destiny, manipulating them toward a death that is not even really death, release, but a kind of limbo state in which the personality "survives" enslaved in the larger force. At the same time, they are linked to the humans themselves, with their hope of escaping the bleakness of the human condition—symbolized by an environment at once dead (inert, lifeless land) and alive (changing, self-destructing). During the final sequence, Corman shows Hank pulling down the tower, a possible means of communication with the outside world, and electrocuting himself along with one of the crabs. In the final shot we see only two survivors—Martha and Dale—trapped on the tiny remains of the island, embracing, but awaiting their inevitable destruction as the island dissolves entirely into the sea.

Not of This Earth

Not of This Earth (1957) is one of Corman's best-known films from the 1950s. He shot it immediately after *Attack of the Crab Monsters* and, in spite of its city setting, it has the same kind of atmosphere as the previous film, an ambience of definite strangeness. The film has structural and thematic links with Corman's other work from this period. Like *Attack of the Crab Monsters* and *War of the Satellites*, it opens with a "teaser" sequence reproduced from the body of the film, designed to stimulate audience interest. Before we know who the characters are or what is happening, we are plunged into *medias res*, watching a middle-aged man sitting in a chair, communicating with a disembodied head about the nature of "earth creatures" and a mysterious "plan" they have concocted. Like *The Day the World Ended* and *Teenage Caveman*, it deals with nuclear destruction, although it somewhat veils this concept by having it occur on another planet, Davanna, from which the lead character, Paul Johnson (Paul Birch), comes. Like *Teenage Doll*, it contains a second initial audience enticement in the form of a written prologue that rolls across the screen. Like the others, it has Corman's characteristic bleak attitude about the pointlessness of life.

Where the film diverges from his other films from this time is in its focusing on a representative of the "other," in this case the deadly ambassador from Davanna. While films like *The Day the World Ended* and *Teenage Caveman* show the clash between the world of "normalcy," of a routineness and regularity that substitutes for true knowledge and the integrated personality, and the abnormal, dangerous, spiritual "other world" that offers the hope of meaning and enlightenment, *Not of This Earth* concentrates almost entirely on the outsider, a man with lethal powers but also an extraordinary weakness. (Corman would later build entire films around this kind of outsider: for example, *X—The Man with the X-Ray Eyes, Bucket of Blood, House of Usher*). Like Usher or Dr. Xavier, Paul Johnson is a paradox—at once powerful, supernaturally so, but also weak, dying in fact, from "evaporating blood." His sensitivity, his place apart from the masses of mankind, is marked by one of his senses being developed to superhuman power. As with other such characters in the Corman gallery, this keenness of sensation has its drawbacks: Johnson's ability to control others with his eyes is balanced by his horror at loud noises. (This becomes particularly important as a way for a character to break his "spell.") Like many of these suicidally brilliant characters—Dr. Xavier, Verden Fell in *Tomb of Ligeia*—Johnson must regulate his own consciousness with the use of extremely dark sunglasses. These serve practically to protect himself from disclosure and others from his power, but, further, as a visual means for the film to separate him from the world of normalcy and link him with the "other" world of mystery and enlightenment.

Not of This Earth echoes *Attack of the Crab Monsters, The Day the World Ended*, and *It Conquered the World* in its use of telepathy as a means of luring the "normal" human being into the clutches of a "monster," an abnormal being who embodies the wantonly destructive nonhuman that the weak human personality is always in danger of becoming. The "desire" to take over people's minds is simply an expression of those minds' already existing predisposition to enslavement, masochism, and self-destruction. Mr. Johnson's physical resemblance to earthlings translates this character into a metaphor for the toppling of the personality from within, since the "monster" is often a destructive wish-fulfillment image for the human being, and "telepathy" is an interiorized, self-derived form of "communication."

The mystery behind Paul Johnson's personality unfolds gradually throughout the film, and he takes on a tragic dimension as his "condition" becomes understood. It seems he has been sent from the planet Davanna to investigate the possibility of utilizing the blood of earthlings, since Davanna has been racked by nuclear wars that have left the blood of its citizens in a continuously evaporating state. Johnson absorbs tremendous amounts of information from reading and analyzing the behavior of those around him, all the while procuring blood from various humans he runs into—a schoolgirl, a salesman, a trio of bums. When he is unable to get what he wants in a peaceful way, he uses mental telepathy to hypnotize his victims into submission, or to kill them if they represent a threat or need. During one of his telepathic speeches to the doctor who is analyzing his blood and trying to

Paul Johnson hides his true personality in Not of This Earth.

help him, he "says," "You will not transmit knowledge of my tragedy." Like other Corman "heroes," Johnson sees himself in a tragic light. His tragedy is that, without constant transfusions, he will die. Though the film shows him frequently killing, it also generates a surprising amount of sympathy for the character, whose dilemma is strongly articulated and felt. Typically, the doctor in the film is his pawn while the female, Johnson's nurse Nadine, representing the life force, the continuity of civilization, refuses to bend her will to his, and upon seeing the mechanism by which he traveled to Earth, wants to destroy it without even knowing what it is.

Not of This Earth is one of Corman's most disturbing and inventive early films. He uses certain structural devices at once resonant and economical. He includes an encounter between Johnson and another Davannan, a woman who has illegally entered the "dimension warp" to escape to Earth with the hope of replenishing her evaporating blood. This encounter is played quite simply, but with an air of strangeness as the distinguishing mark of this pair is the extremely dark sunglasses both wear. Corman follows them along a street, as they stop at a newsstand, seeming half aware of each other, half interested in the magazines. No dialogue exists, except in an overdub that details their telepathic conversation. Johnson is at first irritated at the woman's abuse of the "dimension warp," but sympathizes with her as she tells him she would have died had she not traveled to Earth. The presence of this mysterious pair in the utterly ordinary, realistic surroundings of Los Angeles, circa 1957, gives the environment itself an air of alienation as they are noticed, then ignored by the "normal citizens" around them. Corman's economical rendering of this scene in the use of a vocal overdub rather than synched dialogue adds a further level of isolation to the pair. Mr. Johnson's inadvertent injection of rabid blood into his friend—"I feel activity in my body," she says—ends the scene on a note of pure tragedy.

At first Johnson's powers seem to contradict his self-portrayal as a tragic figure. Once he has hired Nadine as his private nurse, his massive paranoia is revealed as he attempts—for her own safety, he says—to lock her inside her room and reminds his helper Jeremy (Jonathan Haze) to "secure all the outside exits." This sense of paranoia gives an indication of the film's major subtext: like *It Conquered the World*, *Not of This Earth* can be seen as a convoluted cold-war melodrama, with Johnson a perfect embodiment of the Eisenhower-era cold-war monster—a "typical" Russian. Johnson's disturbing individuality is indicated early by his use of opaque sunglasses, implying hidden aspects in his personality that would be revealed by their removal (indeed, this occurs in key scenes in the film, as Johnson removes them to destroy or hypnotize a threatening character). This individuality is contrasted with the buoyantly conformist, easy, comical normalcy of Nadine and her cop boy friend—like the "pods" in Siegel's *Invasion of the Body Snatchers*, these characters can be done in by their inherently conformist nature, with Johnson symptomatic of the "illness" of human homogenization. Johnson is not only individualized, he is inhuman: a scientific personality (Nadine calls him "brilliant") whose colossal absorption of knowledge seems to preempt "Western" humanitarian values. His dispassionate, "objective" view of life is revealed when he tells Nadine, "Death is not a remarkable thing," yet the film compounds his personality by contrasting such a statement with Johnson's desperate attempts to save himself.

The idea of Johnson as a sort of quasi-Russian of the 1950s is furthered during several conversations in the film. When the doctor says, "God forbid such a dreadful new plague should strike the earth" (speaking of the evaporation of blood he sees in Johnson), Johnson shows his scorn for the concept of religion by sarcastically saying, "Yes, God forbid." When Nadine's boy friend says, "Johnson's some kind of foreigner, isn't he?" Nadine replies, "He's got an accent, but I can't place it." The accent with which Johnson speaks is noticeably Eastern European/Russian.

The American view of Russia as a systematic destroyer of freedom, liberty, and individuality—ironically, the very characteristics the film does not emphasize in Nadine, the doctor, or the cop—is furthered during Johnson's communications to those on his home planet. The investigation and possible destruction of Earth is planned in six precisely defined stages: the aliens, like the Russians as portrayed in 1950s popular mythology, will work "phase by phase"; and the destruction of Earth will occur, according to their plan, regardless of whether or not the earthlings' blood can actually be used by the Davannans. At first this seems to be a careless, *wrong* detail, since it would not make sense to have a dying planet destroy Earth whether or not it could "pasture" and bleed its citizens. But seen in terms of the film's subtext of Johnson and his fellow aliens as representing cold-war Russia, this detail does make sense, the ruthlessness of the "enemy" being such that they will destroy Earth regardless of the results of their investigation, out of sheer murderous impulse. Even Johnson's name is a perfect, unmistakably American disguise.

Like many of Corman's collaborations with Griffith, *Not of This Earth* successfully mixes humorous and horrific elements. A seemingly comic bit of business between an obnoxiously persistent vacuum salesman (Dick Miller) and Mr. Johnson begins on a funny note, and ends with a brutal closeup of Johnson shoving the salesman's body into the furnace in his basement. Johnson's encounter with a trio of singing, drunken bums whom he invites to dinner ends gruesomely as Johnson kills each one for his blood. Many of these brief encounters are elliptical, ending with an almost clinical shot of blood racing through the plastic tubes that Johnson carries around in a small suitcase.

As in *It Conquered the World*, the final, important encounter occurs between two beings who express the extremes of their culture: Johnson, a dying vampiric force that must destroy those around him in order to live, and Nadine, who embodies the virtues of wholesomeness and health (it is not accidental that she is a nurse), and, most particularly, the continuance of the race. *Not of This Earth* contains this link with another, later Corman film, *The Last Woman on Earth*, which puts the ultimate decision about world-destruction or world-continuance into the hands of the woman. Nadine's categoric rejection of Johnson and all he stands for goes even farther than that of her boy friend who, as a policeman, could be expected to express a more extreme revulsion at the threat of this alien. But Nadine bears responsibility for articulating the film's positive strivings toward coherence, totality, and life. Typically, she is nearly killed, coming so close to death at the hands of the desperate Johnson that she is standing in his dimension warp when he accidentally veers off the road and kills himself. At John-

son's funeral, her boy friend says, "In a way, I feel sorry for him."
Nadine quickly replies, "I don't." Nadine is as ruthless in her defense
of culture and life as Johnson in his need to destroy it. The film's refusal
to validate completely Nadine's view becomes apparent in the long last
shot. Nadine and her boy friend are talking at the gravesite, but there
is a space between them, and a dark figure walking toward them. As
they continue to talk the figure gets closer and closer, until it is revealed as another Davannan, dressed identically to Johnson and, not
surprisingly, wearing the same ultrathick sunglasses that will protect
him from those around him and vice versa.

3

Criminality and Anxiety

CORMAN DIRECTED FOUR "pure" gangster films during his career, though criminal behavior as a manifestation of philosophical despair finds expression in most of his films, in genres as disparate as science fiction (*The Day the World Ended*), horror (*The Masque of the Red Death*), black comedy (*Bucket of Blood*), and the teen exploitation film (*Teenage Doll*).

Corman made an equal number of westerns early in his career, and the difference in his attitude toward what many consider to be similar—male action—genres is instructive. With the director's interest in ritualized behavior, the influence of the past, and apparently dying genres, one might assume the western would hold a strong attraction for Corman. But *Five Guns West*, *Apache Woman*, *The Oklahoma Woman*, and *The Gunslinger* are among his least personal films.

Both westerns and gangster films can be considered in some sense "male genres," embodying the struggle to achieve patriarchy on a national (western) or personal (the gangster film) scale. Both detail the struggle of an individual (or group acting as a single consciousness) to achieve selfhood or success in a hostile, sometimes incomprehensible environment. Both genres are noted for the obsessively "masculine" orientation of their best-known directors: Ford, Hawks, Boetticher, and Mann. Indeed, these directors have been criticized for the creation of female characters indistinguishable from the men (Hawks), or for the virtual elimination of the female from the world of the films (Mann).

Corman, on the other hand, has shown a definite distaste for strong male characters; even those who occupy center stage in his films tend to be weak or impotent, overcome by a sense of their own failing powers (Roderick Usher, Walter Paisley, Machine Gun Kelly). Corman's entire career can be seen as a subversion of that notion of patriarchy on which both westerns and gangster films are based. Hawks's beloved "camaraderie" does appear in Corman's work, but in a curious inversion the "comrades" are usually female (*Swamp Women*, *Teenage Doll*). In films that do feature male groups, they are usually fronted by wom-

(Top) Shelley Winters as Ma Barker, making her last stand in Bloody Mama; *(bottom) "Without his gun he was naked yellow!"—Charles Bronson in* Machine Gun Kelly.

en (*Machine Gun Kelly, Bloody Mama*). Moral choices, decisions that affect the future of the group or the race, can reside in either male or female, but the male, often motivated by petty self-interest, hubris, or a damaged ego, usually makes the wrong choice. It is up to the woman to attain salvation (rather than patriarchy) on an epic scale (*The Undead, The Last Woman on Earth*).

Corman has commented on this question in reference to *Bucket of Blood:* "It may be that personally I rebel against the concept of the hero." This rebellion, quite evident in the films, caused him to reject many of the conventions of the genres in which he worked. Even in a "typical," that is, male dominated, crime film, Corman undercuts any heroic notions of character by refusing to treat Capone, Moran, or the Gusenbergs with the slightest romanticism or sympathy. Their brutality is presented with graphic bluntness, without the moralism or idolatry we commonly associate with such films.

Corman's embracing of the gangster film, his energetic depiction of both individuals and groups committed to dismantling society, contrasts with his detachment from the westerns, which concern the attempt to build rather than destroy. Although Corman cannot believe in the possibility of a return to "the garden" or "paradise," or a "time of innocence," he nevertheless focuses on the frequent attempts by individuals and groups to destroy what they view as a hopeless, dead culture.

Teenage Doll

Teenage Doll (1957) was Corman's first juvenile delinquency melodrama, based on a screenplay by the director's long-time collaborator, Charles Griffith, at the behest of the same New Orleans theater owners, the Woolner Brothers, who financed an earlier role-reversal melodrama, *Swamp Women.* Like many of Griffith's scripts, *Teenage Doll* capitalizes on the headlines of the day—in this case, increasing gang violence among teenagers. The Woolners' involvement in the project did not extend beyond suggesting an idea and financing it. And, without wishing to minimize Griffith's contribution to the final film, we can say that Corman's manipulation of the formal and thematic elements marks the sixty-eight minute *Teenage Doll* as a masterpiece-in-miniature.

Corman frequently used cartoon or ink wash images during the credit sequences of his films from the 1950s. The obvious point of this is financial: the utter cheapness of relatively static drawn images. (As he increased his budgets and the "importance" of his projects, he abandoned this approach entirely.) A closer look at these "simple" images, however, shows how closely they mirror the film's concerns. In *Machine Gun Kelly*, garish cartoon faces appear, accompanied by jangling pseudoperiod music. In the last seconds before the film proper begins, bullet holes annihilate the faces, this change punctuated by staccato blasts from a horn in the background. In *Teenage Doll*, which has little in the way of comedy, the titles appear on a somber background of gray and black ink washes, frozen images of urban scenes with the "dolls" of the title shown moving through them, sometimes jerking like puppets, sometimes being moved along the backgrounds with utter stiffness.

This poetic opening immediately yields to the film's disclaimer, a note to the audience written on the screen that says the movie is "about a sickness" affecting modern society. "What happened to the girl is unimportant . . . what happens to the rest of society is the most important thing."

Such disclaimers are common enough in film, and often appear as an obligatory nuisance item to be stated and forgotten, a device that offers brief evidence of the filmmaker's social conscience. Not only does this disclaimer have little relevance to the film it precedes, but Corman contradicts it completely by showing the "rest of society" as an entity hardly worth emulating. The film abounds with parent figures, but it shows them as dictatorial (Mr. Bonnie), weak (Hel's father), insane (Mrs. Bonnie), or oblivious/absent (the rest).

The film contains two central images to which it frequently returns. The first is the fatalistic opening image: a dead girl in white lying on a black, rainsoaked street. In a conceit reminiscent of Samuel Fuller, a man in an apron leaves his store and unwittingly throws a pan of dirty dishwater on her prone body. The other image, the thread of the film, is the living girl, Barbara Bonnie, who spends the whole film running to escape the friends of the girl she "accidentally killed." The dead girl was Nan Baker, a member of a gang called "The Black Widows." Barbara, on the other hand, is a "good girl," not a gang member, but involved because she has fallen in love with Eddie, the leader of "The Vandals," with whom Nan Baker was also in love.

Barbara provides the film's focus as a middle-class girl who "stepped out of her class," but each of her pursuers from the Black Widows has a sharply etched scene that tells us everything we need to know about her. The film provides a brief glimpse of each girl's "home life." Far from being havens, their homes are merely houses with a feeling of sordidness, claustrophobia, and estrangement. Lorrie (Sandy Smith) lives in what appears to be a hovel, with garbage strewn throughout and a grimy crippled sister in a ragged dress who begs for "Breakfast, Lorrie, breakfast!" Far from being sentimental, the image is as dis-

The two central images from Teenage Doll: *(top) a running girl (Fay Spain);
(bottom) a dead one.*

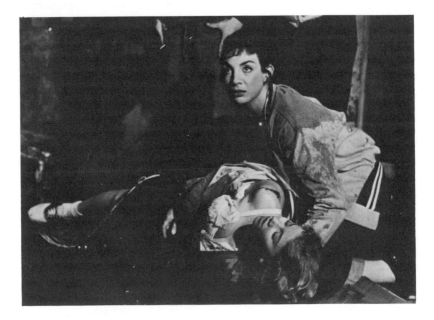

turbing as that of Nan Baker's dead body, particularly when Lorrie
screams at the child, threatens her, then hands her breakfast in the
form of a box of crackers.

Next we see another Black Widow, May (Colette Jackson) in conversation with her sister, Janet (Barboura Morris). Though Janet is a
secretary who trades dates with her "disgusting old boss" for a chance
to escape the "hole" the two of them occupy, Corman uses mirror shots
here to emphasize that they are really variations of the same person,
but at different stages. Both are bitter and cynical, but May is also
hopeless. "Neither of us is going to make it, but you're going to try,"
she says, stating one of the film's major motifs: derision at ambition.

In a scene with tremendous visual force, Corman introduces the
home life of the Black Widows' leader, Hel (Fay Spain). Like the others, she has returned home only to get enough money (or saleable
items) to buy a gun to kill Barbara. She encounters her father embracing another woman while her mother is at work. The woman—hardly
delineated—disappears into the background and the father reiterates
his claims of being too ill to work. Spain is ruthless in criticizing him:
"Who could care about a slob like you?" After an eloquent tirade (during which she has extorted some money from him), she disappears.
The woman who left his embrace earlier returns like an apparition—a
dark outline that, left physically undefined, attains a mythic force as
the embodiment of forbidden pleasure.

The introduction of unsatisfactory or nonexistent parent-child relations prepares us for an alternative in Barbara's home. Briefly, on the
surface, it does seem different. Here we have an integrated family, two
parents and a daughter, a plush-bourgeois home, well-lit and well-appointed (after the chaotic images of hovels and slums seen earlier). But
something is radically wrong here. Barbara's father appears overly
strict, overly concerned with behavior, and her mother, an old woman
wearing pigtails and a teenage party dress, looks and acts insane. Mrs.
Bonnie (whom one of the Vandals later refers to as Barbara's "freak
mother") instantly aligns herself with Barbara, who has returned home
with Nan Baker's blood on her dress. But it is more than parental sympathy that binds them—both live under the tyranny of Mr. Bonnie, a
man blind to the frailties that comprise a human being. He "believes"
her story that a piece of meat (!) fell off a truck and hit her, but only
because he feels as *his* daughter she is incapable of making a wrong
decision.

Far from finding refuge in her own home, Barbara hurries to escape
this estranged environment, to return to Eddie (John Brinkley), the
gang leader who inadvertently caused the crime. Somehow eluding
the girl-gang dragnet, Barbara arrives at the Vandals' clubhouse in the
midst of an auto junkyard. This clubhouse is unusual, however, in that

it is situated underground, with gang members entering by lowering themselves in a small cage controlled by ropes and pulleys. The symbolic potential for this device as an entry into the unconscious, the hidden motive, the "truth," is fully exploited by Corman and Griffith as Barbara's encounter with the club members clarifies her situation as much as it frightens her. When she disclaims responsibility for the death of the girl, Eddie quickly implicates her by saying, "You stepped out of your class." She also learns that he is not in love with her, as he had told her, but was merely using her for sex.

In one of the film's most unsettling moments, the gang members leave, and Barbara is alone with her "guard," Wally (Jay Sayer). Their encounter begins on a solicitous note, with Wally doing most of the talking, urging Barbara to "let it out," saying he knows she is a "good kid" and that she should not be ashamed of crying. His urgings take on a more frantic note as his voice rises, and he begins to implicate her, finally saying the crime occurred because she wanted it to (whether or not she "actually did it")—"Your unconscious mind killed Nan Baker! Oh wow!" he screams, holding his head hysterically. Wally's individual identity disintegrates as he becomes the accusing mirror of her unconscious. Her refusal to acknowledge her own guilt causes her to break a bottle over his head and escape through the cage-elevator. This scene recalls an earlier moment when Barbara encountered a blind man who seemed to "know" she committed a crime—another encounter with the unconscious that triggered Barbara's flight.

The film's major set-piece—the fight between the Vandals and the Tarantulas (the latter the male counterpart of the Black Widows)—follows quickly, and Barbara again manages to escape. Corman switches from the violent encounter in the auto junkyard to an extremely high angle shot of the tiny figure of Barbara running again through the bleak industrial landscape we saw her in earlier. Corman interrupts this with a shot of Mr. Bonnie, followed by a shot of Officer Dunston (Richard Devon). Corman has contrived to position them in exactly the same area of the frame, so that the cut gives the effect of Mr. Bonnie dissolving into the policeman, an extremely inventive way of showing the authoritarian nature of the parent as well as the shifting nature of identity.

Barbara enters a warehouse and is seen by the Black Widows. Eddie is waiting inside, and offers her three "alternatives": "You've got to make up your own mind," he says. "You're lucky you've still got a choice." First, he says, she can let the Black Widows get her, risking death at their hands; second, she can turn herself over to the cops and "die in the gas chamber"; third, she can let him help her get to Phoenix where she will have to change her identity. Typically, the film's "alternatives" are hardly that, since each may involve the literal (the first and second) or symbolic (the third) death of the character. She chooses to give herself up, to risk prison or even "the gas chamber" in order to stop running. Her example is followed by two of the Black Widows, who opt to return to their families, while the others remain behind.

Machine Gun Kelly

Machine Gun Kelly (1958), Corman's first foray into the gangster genre, occupies a special place in the director's career, being the first film to bring him recognition, particularly from European critics who paid attention to him from that point on. The film succeeds as a straight action genre piece, as a groundbreaking portrayal of the gangster as a complex mass of neuroses, and as an examination of criminality as a response to sexual and existential anxiety.

The film emphasizes both the exciting lure that criminality holds for his characters, and the ultimate hopelessness of their situation, in the cartoonish precredit sequence. Roughly drawn faces of the principal characters appear, backed by jangling, upbeat period music. As the credits draw to a close the music changes to blaring horn sounds that accent the visual image of bullet holes ripping open the cartoon faces.

Corman's economic use of his resources is evident in the opening scene, a bank robbery shot in the oblique style common to low-budget films. Unable to afford a bank interior, Corman instead shot the entire scene from just outside, using visual means—tight editing and framing, the shadow of a bank guard with raised hands becoming an image of the real man falling as he is shot, a hand thrust through the glass door of the bank as a siren goes off—to add life to the scene.

The curiously complex relations between the two principals of the film—Flo (Susan Cabot) and George "Machine Gun" Kelly (Charles Bronson)—become clear shortly after the successful robbery. This is our first view of Flo and George, and it appears as a classic mother-son encounter, though the two are obviously lovers. George laughs childishly about the bank robbery and Flo seems irritated and condescending. George criticizes Flo, but from the position of a dependent or victim: "You know, kitten, I'm going to give you a white mouse to play with."

Flo's teasing sexuality is a constant source of torment for Kelly. During an early encounter with the police, Flo's reactions irritate Kelly. He tells her, "Stop calling me cute names and showing your garters." Kelly's fear of sexuality is stated almost baldly when he says to Flo, "Something soft can choke you right into a soft death." Kelly's sexual fears foreshadow the Poe heroes; indeed, he resembles them in more ways than one. Kelly's sexual paranoia is tied up with an equally obsessive, phobic reaction to death. *Machine Gun Kelly* gives about

equal time to these elements in his character, making Kelly one of the
most complexly neurotic characters in Corman's gallery. Flo uses sex
both real and teasing to control Kelly and reinforce his paranoia.

Though the nominal head of his gang, Kelly is a curiously fragile
man. "Afraid of nothing living," Flo says, and the literal correctness of
her statement is apparent when we realize that Kelly is so fearful of
death that he becomes paralyzed in the presence of a coffin or a skull
tattoo. When Flo and Kelly hide out at Flo's parents' house (a whorehouse), Kelly's relaxed responses end abruptly when he notices a skull
tattooed on Flo's father's hand. Later, when one of his gang members,
Howard, shows him an "icon" he is carving and says it represents the
"god of death," Kelly loses control and almost kills Howard. Kelly is
unquestionably powerful, but also intensely insecure. Flo shows her
thorough understanding of Kelly, and summarizes the contradictions
in his personality, by calling him "my boss-baby."

Kelly is threatened and tormented by all the characters around him.
Unable to command loyalty, he is harassed even by members of his
own gang. He is surrounded by symbolically castrated "half-men," including Harry (Frank de Kova), who has only one good arm, Fanny
(Morey Amsterdam), one of the film's two gay characters, and the "aesthete" Howard (Jack Lambert). The first encounter we see between
Kelly and Harry involves a threat by Harry to release a caged mountain
lion to kill Kelly. Our first view of Fanny is memorable for Fanny's
blatant attempt to pocket some of the bank money.

Kelly is perceived as weak in spite of his abilities with the gun. Flo's
mother takes an instant dislike to him, constantly upbraiding him in
the presence of others. She refers to him as "it," "that," and "big baby,"
and ridicules him for not being able to "crack a hick town bank," after
he bungles a job.

The concept of the jungle underlies the entire film. Our first view
of Flo shows her wearing elaborate furs—not in the form of coats,
which tend to disguise their origin, but fox carcasses, which she drapes
over her shoulders. At one point Kelly tells her, "You like to be pet-
ted. . . ." Harry's obsession with animals, with "the big kill," is contrasted with his crippled condition, the result of a "mauling" by a "big
cat" that Kelly laughingly insists "came out of a bottle." And one of the
most powerful elements in the film is the caged mountain lion that
Harry keeps on the premises of his gas station. This beast is instru-
mental in several scenes: in demonstrating Kelly's trauma when Harry
removes the lock; in the mauling of Fanny; in a scene where Kelly
spits soda pop into the cat's face; in Corman's dissolve into this image
after Kelly kills Howard, as a symbol of Kelly's (temporary) reassertion
of control, his ability to tap his own animal power.

Kelly's death obsession begins to overwhelm him in the latter half of the film. In a particularly striking scene, he is walking toward a bank in preparation for another robbery. The job has been planned in great detail, and requires pinpoint timing. But Kelly's walk is interrupted by some delivery men carrying a coffin to a building. Kelly becomes temporarily frozen, then engages in a clumsy, dancelike movement with the coffin reminiscent of an uncertain encounter between two strangers on the street, where it is unclear who will yield the right of way. Kelly's paralysis throws off the timing, the bank job is botched, and he becomes more vulnerable to the ambitious members of his group.

Corman dramatizes this and many of the scenes as brief, incisive set-pieces. The mauling of Fanny is shown elliptically, with Fanny and Kelly engaged in nervous dialogue beside the caged cat: "George, sometimes you don't make any sense." Kelly baits Fanny, then grabs him and shoves his head down toward the cage. We learn later that Fanny, like Harry, has "lost his arm," another of the film's several symbolic castrations.

The encounter between Fanny's friend, Philip Ashton, and Flo, is played in a stylized manner, with gestures replacing generalized, "realistic" behavior. Corman also shoots the scene in which Kelly "plays" with one of the girls in Flo's mother's whorehouse in a wholly unrealistic style, for maximum psychological effect. Kelly and the girl are rolling around on the floor, kissing and hugging—but the lack of real sexuality between them is underscored by Kelly's comic-ironic statement that "It's all right, because it's all in the family." When Flo arrives she interrupts the girl's mock-seductive dance before Kelly, and Corman freezes the scene with a high/low angle cut between the girl she has thrown to the floor (we did not see this happen), and Flo's striking image. When Flo slaps Kelly, he slaps her back, but Flo has her revenge by forcing Kelly to admit his dependent, childish role. She also makes him admit his weakness, his fear of death: "Tell me, George, you were scared, weren't you?"

Kelly's external ruthlessness and interior weakness is perceived even by the nurse he kidnaps. "You're a little too young for giant steps, aren't you?" she says, in spite of his menacing talk and the presence of the machine gun. His plot to kidnap the daughter of a steel magnate is foiled by the arrival of Flo's parents, who barge in loaded with toys and food for the child, and turn aside Kelly's attempts to make them leave.

In *Machine Gun Kelly* there is a conscious link between anxiety and criminality that appears only sporadically in *Bloody Mama* and not at all in *The St. Valentine's Day Massacre*. The latter film, in particular,

shows criminal behavior as an almost natural, animal response to the
perceived weakness of society, its need to self-destruct. The criminals
in *Bloody Mama* embody an element of chaos (Corman called the
group "basically pre-civilization") and an attempt to achieve power and
identity through antisocial behavior. The criminality in Flo and Kelly
derives from Flo's impulse to dominate, to have the godlike power of
creation and destruction and from Kelly's sexual anxiety, which he am-
plifies through his association with Flo.

Flo's sexual torment of Kelly runs throughout the film. She flirts
with other men, all other men, from Howard to Harry to an unseen
bank teller. Kelly's sexual anxieties seem to be verified when Flo's teasing of these characters shortly precedes their deaths. Though, as Flo
says, "Machine Gun Kelly is my little baby . . . best gun of them all,"
his gun is no match for her power, and his occasional outbursts are
taken in stride by Flo, who wants to succeed in her chosen business
and uses Kelly to gain her ends—the ultimate double-crossing
"Mother."

Shortly before he is caught, Kelly awakens from a nightmare in
which he has seen himself in a coffin. Corman punctuates this by showing him in the claustrophobic lower half of a bunk. By the time the
police arrive, he is reduced almost to tears—"I never wanted any of
it!"—while Flo is still ready to fight. It is not until Kelly admits pub-
licly his weakness—a revelation accompanied significantly by the
deaths of two of his chief tormentors, the two cripples Fanny and Harry, that Kelly's anxiety dissipates. The police put the final humiliating
touch on the matter by calling him "Pop-Gun Kelly," and Corman ends
the film on a ruthless note with a close-up of Kelly's gun.

A Bucket of Blood

A Bucket of Blood (1959) is perhaps Corman's most effective, certainly his bleakest pre-Poe film. It ranks with *The Day the World Ended* and *Teenage Doll* (the latter an equally brilliant Charles Griffith
script) as perhaps the best of his early genre efforts. The genre is the
familiar one of the "little man," the scorned, seemingly sexless character who exacts an elaborate revenge on his tormentors—society at
large—by assuming a new identity, traveling from one level of society
to another through some violent act. Ostensibly a comedy, the film's
humor is almost entirely gruesome, based on a grim awareness of the
gulf between people, the isolation of the individual, the impossibility
of satisfaction or pleasure or faith. In addition, *Bucket of Blood*
emerges as the most intense pre-Poe self-portrait Corman committed
to film.

Walter Paisley (Dick Miller) is a painfully inarticulate busboy and waiter at a hipster club, "The Yellow Door." His need to belong, even to a hollow group like the Beatniks, is powerful, but Walter's clumsiness and seeming stupidity elicit reactions of amusement, condescension or indifference from the people around him. He covets one of the women, Carla (Barboura Morris), obviously beyond his grasp, as well as the approval of the group.

Corman establishes the film's theme of dominance/submission with the first shot in the film: a low-angle closeup of one of the Beatniks at "The Yellow Door" reciting senseless poetry to a blasé audience. As Maxwell Brock (Julian Burton) is reciting lines like "Life is an obscure hobo, bumming a ride on the omnibus of art . . .," the camera slowly tracks backward to reveal the detailed, insular environment of the club, and the hunched-over, self-apologizing figure of the busboy collecting his cups with a grim smile. Brock stands on a stage far above Walter, but he is "above" the busboy in every sense—the ultimate hollow hipster who uses verbal paradox to delineate and cruelly control an entire self-enclosed world. His opening words subordinate life to "art":

> Let us talk of art.
> For there is nothing else to talk about.
> For there is nothing else.

These lines foreshadow the film's ruthless view of an empty, fake world in which art—stylization, ultimately death—prevails. Accepted, even idolized, Brock is the chief spokesman for the group, who hang on his every word, no matter how obscure or contradictory. He is also one of several of the film's targets, the single character most blamed by the film for what happens to Walter. Brock's smug cynicism is thorough: "Repetition is death," he pontificates to his rapt audience. When he congratulates himself for the fact that his poetry is understood "only by that minority which is aware," one of the women asks, "Aware of what?" She is quickly ridiculed by one of the perhaps more aware characters: "Not aware of anything, stupid! Just aware." Brock's harping on his own enlightenment reveals a supercilious, empty character, but one deified by Walter, who commits to memory all of Brock's poems and takes them so much to heart that he eventually both uncovers Brock's hypocrisy *and* uses Brock's words literally as an excuse for his murderous acts.

Walter's alternative to the glittering "aware" club is his sordid, depressing apartment, where he lives alone. The only human contact he seems to have away from the club is his landlady, a matronly busybody who enforces Walter's sexless life-style by constantly reminding him that he cannot bring girls to her "respectable rooming house," in reality a rotting tenement. (Walter is not the only character who is not "aware.") This unsatisfactory mother figure is the closest Walter comes to any kind of family situation, except for the imaginary world at "The Yellow Door."

Goaded into pretending he too is an artist—"I'm working on something . . . it's not finished yet"—Walter gets a block of clay with which to make his first "sculpture." His faltering, frustrated attempts to mold the lifeless clay into something "artistic" or even recognizably human are painful to watch. Corman forces us to confront the character's hopelessness by shooting the scenes of Walter's awkward attempts to be an artist in extremely long takes. Using a photograph of Carla for inspiration, Walter pushes and pulls on the clay, growing more and more agitated by the clay's stubborn refusal to cooperate: "Be a nose . . . be a nose!" he screams. In the lonely environment of his mind, however, his prayers are answered: the landlady's lost cat has trapped itself inside his wall, and is crying. Walter trips through the room, burns his hand on a boiling pot, sets the overhead light bulb swinging in a wide arc, and arrives, knife in hand, to "save" the cat from its imprisonment. The similarities between Walter's condition and the cat's are clear: both are "trapped" personalities, both are inarticulate, "misunderstood." Walter's attempt to free the cat is a typical miscalculation on his part: attempting to cut into the wall, he inadvertently stabs and kills the cat. At first genuinely sorry, Walter realizes during a reverie that the cat can serve a useful purpose, providing him with the "artwork" he needs to impress the hipsters. He covers the dead animal with clay and passes it off as a modern sculpture. He improvises a startlingly direct name: "Dead Cat."

Walter's wish-fulfillment act offers the hope of a radical change in status. This change appears initially superficial, however. Both Leonard (Antony Carbone), the club owner, and Brock, the pretentious poet, end their praise of his sculpture "Dead Cat" by telling him to get back to his work as busboy/janitor/waiter. Walter succeeds immediately with the one person he most wanted to impress—Carla, who acclaims it a "masterpiece"—and the rest of the club habitués echo her reaction. One of the girls, Naolia, reveals the vampiric aspect of the hangers-on: "Walter, I wanna be with you . . . you're *creative!*"

Walter's second "murder" is also both accidental and the product of a wish-fulfillment fantasy. Naolia's desire to "be with" Walter is rebuffed because Walter is afraid of his landlady's reaction, so Naolia instead gives him some heroin. Walter doesn't know what it is, and sets it on his kitchen table next to the clay. Unbeknownst to him, an undercover agent has watched this exchange and goes to Walter's apartment to arrest him. Told the "stuff" is "heroin, horse," Walter is comically oblivious: "Gee, wasn't it nice of Naolia to give me that expensive horse?" The unamused agent threatens Walter, who slices open his head with a pancake skillet. Thus his second sculpture is born: "Murdered Man."

Walter's increasingly active inner life, his increasing suspension of social rules to achieve what he wants, is noted by the landlady right after this murder. Suspicious by nature, she says, "Walter, have you been talking to yourself again?" He replies, "Well, I guess maybe I have, Mrs. Swickert. Somebody's got to." Corman again shows the pathetic nature of this character, who has to invent companions to avoid alienation, and who must kill the people around him in order to destroy the coldness they represent and, simultaneously, to merge with them. Walter's destruction of the cat and the undercover cop represent his attempts to leave behind his old personality, to alter an unacceptable identity that holds him in a state of loneliness and misery. The somberness of his situation is further emphasized in the shot that immediately follows his second murder: a folksinger at "The Yellow Door" is singing a minor-key song with the words, "Go down, you murderer, go down!" as Walter enters the frame, again oblivious.

Walter is finally achieving on his own what Maxwell Brock has been doing throughout the film: creating a world that derives exclusively from his own personality, an embittered, unevolved personality that sees others as frozen, unresponsive, mutilated, or dead statues. These "artworks" also attest to Walter's inability to adapt to, succeed at life. As he assumes control, Walter changes visually. He enters the club not to work, but to sit and be waited on. His costume becomes both a general satire of the artist of popular mythology (beret, loud jacket, neck scarf, cigarette holder) and a specific doubling of the image of the club owner, Leonard—significantly, the first person to realize that his statues are actually murder victims covered with clay. Brock's admiration for Walter has grown, as has Carla's. In the latter case, however, Walter's stupidity again arises as he interprets a simple kiss from her as a declaration of lifelong love.

The film becomes more ruthless in its portrayal of the empty world of the Beats. We have already seen that the group contains within itself the seeds of self-destruction in the form of several undercover cops who spend all their time there, waiting to bust the owner or habitués. This emptiness is again emphasized as a beautiful, pretentious model named Alice (Judy Bamber) arrives at the club to torment Walter with her unobtainable sexuality. She has just returned from Big Sur where she "went to look for Henry Miller" (she did not find him) and is appalled to find "the busboy!" sitting at a table with "sophisticated Beatniks!" She is particularly vicious to Walter, whom she refers to as "a simple farmboy," claiming that the "whole thing"—the "charade" of

Dick Miller as Walter Paisley mimics the popular stereotype of "the artist" in A Bucket of Blood.

Walter-as-artist—is being staged for her benefit. Walter's new confidence (and his unintentional humor) emerges during this scene as Alice challenges him to make a sculpture out of a piece of cheesecake. He smashes it in her hand and calls it "Hand!" to the amusement of the Beats. (Like the simple names Walter chooses for his "sculptures," his calling the smashed cheesecake "Hand" shows how simply, directly he sees life.) At this point Walter abandons the "accidental" aspect (self-defense) of his killing in favor of a satisfaction of the revenge impulse. Alice's sexual torment provides Walter with his motive, and Alice becomes his third sculpture as he strangles her and puts her on display with the previous pair.

By now Walter is almost completely out of control—alienated from the group in spite of his elevation to the role he desperately sought. He begs Carla to marry him and she, unwilling to consider the man as anything but an object of pity (pre-artist) or detached admiration (artist), rejects him. Walter recognizes Brock for the hollow man he is, as Brock congratulates him and says, "You can make $25,000 on these pieces alone." Walter bitterly replies, "I thought you put money down." Brock says, "I do, but 25 *thou!*" Walter mulls over Brock's poetry in his mind: "People become clay in his [the artist's] hands that he might mold them. . . ." This phrase is the most conscious link between Walter's murderous activities and Brock's cynical attitudes, the murders an acting-out, a logical extension of Brock's inhuman words.

Walter's logic is always his own, however, consistent to the end. The same personality that destroyed the cat and three people to provide his ticket to social acceptance—"art"—is the one that could, upon discovery, retreat to his room and say, "I'll hide where they'll never find me." His solution is the logical one of merging with his radical, highly appreciated artworks—covering his body with clay and hanging himself.

Bucket of Blood is one of Corman's grimmest films, certainly the most depressing comedy in his work. It is also one of his most personal, as the film encourages a reading of Walter Paisley as a double for the director. Certainly, Corman can be seen to exist in many of his films; the usual representation is the supersensitive aesthete of the Poe films or the scientific personality of *X—Man with the X-Ray Eyes*. The distinguishing characteristic of these men is their creation of an enclosed world which they control—temporarily—as an alternative to the unacceptable "real" world whose chief characteristic is eventual death. Corman's films represent the same kind of creation in their obsession with environment as an expression of personality, with enclosure as both a protection for personality and that personality's undoing. Normally these creators—Roderick Usher, Dr. Xavier—are, like Corman, extremely articulate, supersensitive, and overcivilized. Part of *Bucket of Blood's* utter bleakness derives from the lack of articulation in its chief character, Walter Paisley. Like Corman, Walter is an "artist," but one who creates "fake art," art that is somehow not real. As with Walter, there is the general belief that Corman is "putting something over on people." Like Corman, Walter creates his work with extraordinary speed; Corman's five-day schedule for *Bucket of Blood* is easily translated into Walter's suspicious overnight "creation" of his figures. Even the gruesome aspects of Corman's films—which abound with monsters both alien and human—are mirrored in Walter's grotesque, frightening statues. Corman's closeness to the material is clear from the deliberate use of long takes and the somewhat uncharacteristic closeups of Walter. The powerful frustrations of the character are continuously expressed in shots that combine these two techniques, particularly during his first attempt to shape the clay, and in the scene where he waits outside Alice's door prior to luring her to her death. The character's Cormanesque self-loathing is emphasized in the final shot, a closeup that recalls the closeup of Brock that began the film, but which this time indicates with devastating finality that Walter Paisley—contrary to Brock's ironic phrase "born"—is dead.

The Intruder

The Intruder (1962) opens with a motif we recognize from the Poe films—the entry of a mysterious outsider into an insular, dying world. Unlike the Poes, however, this "world" is the real one, the racially polarized South circa 1960. Corman films the arrival of Adam Cramer (William Shatner) in a typically graceful but detached way: the camera, anchored in a bus driving into a small, sleepy Southern town, assumes Cramer's point of view, casually surveying the images that comprise it: aging storefronts, a few scattered citizens. The immediate impression is one of backwardness; the town is clinging to values the larger society must consider outmoded and dangerous, and Cramer arrives as a deus ex machina to try to preserve the fragile identity of the town against the onslaught of historic progression.

Our first view of Cramer himself occurs when the bus stops and, typically, the stranger who steps forward is wearing opaque sunglasses, signaling his similarity to other Corman "heroes" who, hiding their true personalities and intentions, are planning an assault on the social or philosophical status quo.

Cramer emerges quickly as a savvy, brash, authoritative character—a sort of "salesman" (as several characters call him) who uses personal charm and solicitousness to gain the confidence of the hotel desk clerk. He emphasizes his individuality, his separation from the rabble, his need to be alone, by telling her he does not wish to be disturbed and will do his own room cleaning. The brutal, depressing tone of the film becomes evident in the initial encounter between the two. The hotel clerk is a stereotypically sweet-looking old lady who, failing to rouse an old man to carry Cramer's bags, says with a little laugh: "I swear that boy's got nigger blood in him." The film undercuts this kind of cliché imagery throughout, playing against expectations of *The Intruder* as simply another Krameresque problem picture. That the old woman is clearly a "real person" and not a professional actress (most of the cast was nonprofessional) further underscores Corman's success at showing the sordidness of "real life."

Cramer, a man obsessed with taking control, instinctively comprehends the power structure of the town, immediately paying a visit to the local patriarch, Verne Shipman (Robert Emhardt). This visit is the first step in Kramer's elaborate plan to both create (to remake the town in his own image) and destroy (to lead the town away from civilization by defying man-made law and order). Cramer's plan is simply to rouse the populace to resist federally imposed integration, by any means possible.

The world of the town is shown in microcosm in the homely interiors of its drug stores, cheap hotels, and, particularly, the immaculate white kitchen of newspaperman Tom McDaniel's (Frank Maxwell) house. This is a sterile, dying world that awaits the chance for revivifying by someone like Cramer. The wrenching conflict within the family is also indicated here, as McDaniel, his wife and daughter, and cantankerous father-in-law argue about the rightness or wrongness of "the law" that says blacks must be allowed to enter the white school. The sense of physical order, emptiness, and conflict contrasts strongly with the view of a typical house in "Niggertown," a house in which cold plushness is replaced by a disordered yet vital environment, with jazz blaring off a radio, and a feeling of warmth and consistency not present in the white house.

Tom McDaniel's movement between these two worlds contrasts with Cramer's. Both are go-betweens, but McDaniel's movement is toward a realization of the similarities between the two (unity, coherence) and the stupidity of the polarization, while Cramer's emphasis of the differences points to his lack of enlightenment, his impulse toward division and conflict. McDaniel is later punished for his insight, his desire to open the town to a modern, more humane way of life, when some embittered townspeople savagely beat him, causing him to lose one eye.

Cramer successfully ingratiates himself with both the powers-that-be and the rabble, but the film shows him as a restless, dissatisfied personality. During a late night encounter with Vi Griffin, Cramer says: "I almost go crazy sometimes because there isn't anybody who feels things the way I do!" On the one hand we can read the comment as his way of eliciting sympathy from Vi, whom he seduces; on the other it simply indicates Cramer's utter estrangement from life, and his desire to "find himself" through large-scale control and defiance of order.

In spite of his power at manipulating the mob he is creating, indicated by Corman in several telling scenes, Cramer seems almost invented by the town as a way of achieving "its status as a closed, homogeneous community," as Paul Willeman put it. Willeman offers the most cogent analysis by emphasizing that neither Cramer nor Sam Griffin, who exposes him (nor for that matter, Tom McDaniel, the other principal in the film), "assumes the central position in the story. . . . They are seen as part of the mechanics of dramatic movement, setting the action in motion and finally terminating it."[1] Cramer's vacillations between pitiable weakness and supernatural power (shown startlingly when he appears from nowhere in Ella McDaniel's room to urge her to claim to have been raped by a black man) leave him as alienated as the townspeople, but he does answer a need in them as much as they provide a temporary antidote for his own problems.

Willeman sees the entire story as not so much political as mythic, with the "sense that the age of love and innocence and happiness [have] . . . long since passed, and without some kind of ritual involving either mental or physical violence, we cannot hope to transcend our condition of isolation."[2] Thus Cramer becomes a tool for the townspeople's conscious desire to rid itself of Northern, civilized, "carpetbagger" influences, and its unconscious desire to recapture the Golden Age, the "garden" that is the distant symbol of happiness in myth and legend. This recapturing involves a ritual purging, here a cleansing of the white race through the lynching of a young black man.

Although much of the story takes place outdoors, Corman uses various means to make the drama archetypal, showing both the desperate town and Adam Cramer as fragile, self-created entities moving alternately toward self-actualization and self-destruction. Corman's camerawork is particularly self-conscious here, constantly calling attention to itself in the surveying tracks and dollies that document the movements of the characters and the locales they inhabit, from Tom McDaniel's house to the shacks of Niggertown, to Verne Shipman's open, airy mansion. One particularly spectacular shot shows Cramer as both victim and victor when, just before one of his dynamic speeches, the camera races toward his sweating, brightly smiling face and ends in a choker closeup, indicating Cramer's (temporary) godlike status.

Like the rest of the town, Sam Griffin is initially seduced by Cramer's charismatic personality, without necessarily subscribing to his racial views. Cramer's inability to suppress his strong, exploitative sexuality leads to a brief liaison with Griffin's wife that recasts Griffin as Cramer's enemy. Cramer's equally brief involvement with Tom McDaniel's daughter is another unnecessary strategic error. In both cases Cramer's secular lust gets in the way of his epic impulses: "Great times call forth great men," he tells Vi. Yet Cramer begins to destroy what he is creating almost as soon as he arrives.

The film's pitiless rendering of the social situation is seen during a montage of the ghostly cavalcade of Ku Klux Klan members burning a cross. This disturbing real footage, however, is immediately related back to Cramer, as Corman cuts to his seduction of Vi Griffin, framing their encounter in a dark hotel room with the blinking light of a neon sign across the street, and dissolving to the image of the burning cross as they make love. Cramer's unloosing of the town's most antisocial impulses is clearly beyond his control, and he spends much of his time reprimanding individual members of his mob for their participation in "stupid acts." Like *Machine Gun Kelly*, Cramer is a leader whose followers are only there temporarily, until they can seize power for themselves or until they have exhausted their own uses for Cramer.

The Intruder is a typically graphic Corman production from the 1960s, opening the way for the blunt portrayals of sexuality and criminality in *The Wild Angels* and *Bloody Mama*. He handles the liaison between Vi and Cramer with intense sensuality, relating their passion visually to the burning cross and the light-dark blinking in the hotel room. In the midst of the epic movements of the aroused mob, Corman focuses briefly on the face of a harassed black man who simply says, "Why?" The reactions of Verne Shipman to the accused rapist Joey Green, to the school principal, to Adam Cramer—all of whom he physically assaults—are treated with unsentimental directness, leaving a sense of distaste and disturbance with the viewer.

All the film's major elements—Cramer's lust for power and loss of control, Ella McDaniel's phony story, Joey Green's near lynching, the mob's cohesion or dispersal, the reassertion of Verne Shipman, the inadequacy of civilized authority to deal with the self-determination of a mob—come together in the film's final sequence in the playground. Willeman is again brilliant in his analysis of this scene, and it deserves to be quoted at length:

Significantly, Cramer is exposed by another stranger, Sam Griffin. The scene of this exposure is set in a playground in front of a school, an ambiguous symbol: the schoolhouse itself standing for reason and culture, the playground performing the function of a safety valve for repressed emotions and instincts. The head of the school finds he finally has to give way to the instinctive urges of the mob, and the lynching is about to take place in the playground. The swing, selected for the exercise, is another such ambiguous symbol, standing simultaneously for childish innocence and primitive savagery, together with a third dimension, the representation of Time, as it swings to and fro like a pendulum. Time, manifested in the swing, becomes inactive, but we know similar forces will inevitably set it in motion again, perhaps in another place, until society's instinctual drives have been satisfied."[3]

The concept of "instincts," of uncontrolled drives, is central to the film. Cramer is a man victimized by his own drives, an intellectual criminal yet highly passionate, so much so that he wrecks his plan to fight the cycle of conformity for the town through liaisons with Vi and Ella, and through misjudging the power of the larger, less controllable instincts of the mob. When it begins to act on its own, the effect spirals and Cramer loses control. He is finally reduced to a sputtering, desperate man ("I saw you kiss a nigger woman!" he says) when Sam Griffin exposes him. Curiously, Griffin does not seem overly bitter, reinforcing the film's rather objective view of Cramer as ultimately weak and unactualized, characteristics Griffin seems to understand and respond to. The film is open-ended as to what will happen next, but it is clear that in spite of the mob's need to use Cramer to express criminal and other socially unacceptable traits, it cannot continue when Cramer is exposed and degraded.

While *The Intruder* is remarkably advanced in its ruthless portrayal of the problems of segregation, it must be considered subversive in more ways than merely social. The film represents a slap in the face at Corman's own highly cultivated audience—the disenfranchised Southerners who comprised a significant part of his audience from the mid-1950s on. It is not accidental that Corman had problems shooting the film once the pro-integration nature of the film became known. Corman's willingness to experiment with what he considered "overt social comment," to risk alienating his audience by repudiating one of their cherished beliefs—the "sanctity" of segregation—was not repeated in his career. Alarmed by the complete commercial failure of the film, Corman returned quickly to the safer, more interiorized dramas of the Poe films.

The St. Valentine's Day Massacre

Cameraman Milton Krasner stressed the "realistic" aspects of Corman's third gangster film, *The St. Valentine's Day Massacre* (1967), in an article in the *American Cinematographer.* "Initial consideration was given to filming the story in Chicago,"[4] he said. Twentieth Century-Fox surveyed the actual locations where the events of the massacre occurred, but found them either "torn down or modernized." According to Krasner, the set designers at Fox then re-created these locales "in meticulous detail" on the sound stages at Fox and the backlot of MGM.

In preparing to shoot the film, Krasner studied "actual news photographs taken immediately after the actual shooting" and used them as a guide to "duplicate realistic lighting and mood of the locale."

Corman, too, has spoken of the film as "perhaps the first totally historic gangster film in the history of Hollywood,"[5] and *Variety* printed one of many reviews congratulating the film's "semi-documentary style."

Certainly, *The St. Valentine's Day Massacre* could be said to render reality by adhering to historical truth. And unlike other gangster biopics of the day (most notably *Bonnie and Clyde*, released the same year), the film avoids glamorizing its subject.

But the "realism" of the film exists primarily on an historical level. Corman's treatment of the material, superficially "semi-documentary," is so self-consciously artful that the film is one of his most controlled, resonant productions. It works both as a straight, "torn-from-the-pages-of-life" gangster film, and as a highly stylized philosophical drama that casts Fate as alternately indifferent and malign.

The film does contain conscious, recognizable documentary elements, most notably in Paul Frees's deadpan overdub, which offers the viewer spoken biographies-in-miniature of the characters. However, even this device serves a deeper function, by encapsulating the person, really trapping him—giving a birth date, a brief, cynical bit of history (of Pete Gusenberg: "His first act upon returning from school to find his mother dead was to pry the wedding ring off her finger"), and the date of his death. The overdub introduces a godlike element, an all-encompassing intelligence that, like the director, stands outside the story proper, denigrating and trivializing the characters, and pointing out with utter matter-of-factness how and when they will die.

Whereas the overdub introduces a mock objectivity into the film (objectivity masking cruel Fate), the camera is used as both an external and internal presence, moving freely through the blood-spattered environment of this enclosed, artificial Chicago, pursuing characters and drawing them to their deaths. Characters walk toward and away from the camera, creating the idea of the camera as a philosophical element, sometimes distant or majestic (the extraordinary opening high crane shot which leads the viewer slowly into the city), sometimes surveying (the celebrated tracking shot over the bloodstained wall of the garage), sometimes as relentlessly pursuing fate. A good example of the latter can be seen in the sequence where Alex d'Arcy is trying to escape from Capone, who knows he helped kill Capone's friend, corrupt religioso/mafia chieftain Patsy Lolordo. D'Arcy leaves the interior train station as the train is starting to leave, and he moves quickly parallel to it.

The camera dollies tremulously backward as D'Arcy moves, drawing him on, closer to where he can enter the train. Once "safe" inside, D'Arcy is killed by Capone, who has entered the train disguised as a ticket collector.

Thus Corman introduces two elements, one "realistic" (the Dragnet-style overdub), one aesthetic (the spectacularly obvious camera), to show the triumph of death over life. The film reinforces this idea with several juxtapositions of a sentimental with a fatalistic image, notably during the death of a gangster in a flower shop and his subsequent lying-in-state in a room filled equally with elaborate floral bouquets and black-clad gangsters.

Such couplings are common in gangster films, going back at least as far as the original *Scarface* (1932). However, Corman's version of the St. Valentine's Day Massacre, while declaring its adherence to genre convention with various homages throughout,[6] seems closer in spirit to some of Corman's nongangster films—the extremely internalized Poe films, *X—Man with the X-Ray Eyes*. Whereas *Machine Gun Kelly* showcases a hero made of equal parts of violence and neurotic fear, the killers in *The St. Valentine's Day Massacre* are utterly ruthless. Straight "society," seen in various incarnations in the earlier film, makes only one significant appearance in *The St. Valentine's Day Massacre*, and that is at the very beginning when Barboura Morris (a Corman favorite) as an average citizen hears gunshots and goes into the garage, registers what happened, and screams long and loud. From this point on, virtually every character is shown as part of the gangster underworld. Even a group of reporters who interview Capone after the massacre are shown as congenial, even fawning on Capone as he regales them with a combination of jokes and harsh words. Everyone is involved in the lawlessness Corman evokes, from the petty garage mechanic who needs the gang's money for his baby, to the accountant who promises his wife "this will be the last time."

As in many Corman films, "characterization" in the classic sense holds little interest. Indeed, this is one of many of his films criticized for its "bad acting," with Jason Robards often singled out as "overacting." Certainly, there is no sense of modulation in the performances, and very little sympathy for the characters is evoked. But why should Corman want to evoke sympathy? Corman's films contain two kinds of criminals: those for whom crime is a response to sexual anxiety or philosophical despair (*Teenage Doll, Machine Gun Kelly, The Wild Angels*), and those who are simply acting out a corrupt civilization's need to self-destruct (*The St. Valentine's Day Massacre, Bloody Mama*). Though Corman's bleak attitudes allow little sympathy for either type, there is virtually none for the latter. The destruction of the inhabitants of *The*

Al Capone (Jason Robards) at the center of chaos in The St. Valentine's Day Massacre.

St. Valentine's Day Massacre is treated as methodically, as "naturally" as their attempts to dismantle society.

The characters in *The St. Valentine's Day Massacre* are reduced to puppets from the outset, with the overdub dismissing them from life. In spite of the film's documentary impulses, these are not rounded, credible people so much as machines of violence, exhibiting behavioral gestures, archetypal "emotions," and enactments of ritual (Capone's unbelievable tearful explanation of his need to kill Bugs Moran based on Moran's killing of Patsy Lolordo; Capone's baseball-bat destruction of two traitorous thugs).

The characters in the film respond to their desire for position—identity—by killing. Introspection does not exist, and the film careens along from one violent episode to another, marching each man toward his death. For these criminals, life is something beyond comprehension. Like animals, they are born, they kill, they die. The presence of society is introduced and dismissed at the beginning in the form of the screaming woman, and reappears briefly in the mock-policemen who help Capone orchestrate the massacre.

Corman emphasizes mood and ambience "at the expense of" acting. In *The St. Valentine's Day Massacre* the mood is determined by the elaborate sets. The sense of fatalism inherent in the plot increases as we note the falseness, the temporary nature of this environment, which exists under a painted sky. The static nature of the characters— incapable of change—is belied by Corman's majestic crane and tracking work, which creates a supplementary dimension outside the film's sordid events. The ending contains some of the most effective camerawork in his career, where the camera tracks along the bloodstained garage wall (a shot reprised by Martin Scorsese in the postmassacre scene in *Taxi Driver*) and dissolves into a montage of striking shots that relate the deaths of most of the principals.

Because the film begins (like *Day the World Ended* or *Teenage Caveman*) "at the end" with the entire film constructed in flashback, all the characters we see as the action unfolds are literally dead when the film begins. Corman perfects this conceit by treating the locales with utter self-consciousness, leaving us with "dead" characters playing out their lives in densely detailed yet obvious studio sets.

Bloody Mama

Bloody Mama (1969) presents one of its central concepts—the violation of innocence in nature—in a brief opening montage. We see a young Kate Barker running through a lush forest. This idyllic image of childish exuberance is soon undercut by the presence of voices— male—and what appears to be an innocent encounter between child and nature becomes a frenzied attempt by the child to avoid being raped. Kate's protests are stifled by her father, who accuses her of not being "hospitable . . . Blood's thicker than water." This ironically beautiful image of incest and rape in a lush natural setting sets the tone for the entire film, which is based on juxtaposing apparently positive values (the cohesion of the family, the beauty, openness, and optimism of the American landscape) with apparently negative ones (murder, rape, incest, drugs). To put it another way, the film casts the Barkers' struggle as an inversion of the American success story, pitting an intensely determined, antisocial, self-motivated, and self-enclosed group against the "civilized society" around them.

In an interview in *Sight and Sound* magazine, Corman described the Barkers as "pre-civilization; they came out of the hills, they were hillbillies, they had certain basic desires and drives that were only slightly modified by civilization. . . ."[7] The group is ruled by a powerful matriarch, the now-grown Kate Barker (Shelley Winters), who has raised four "fine sons," Herman (Don Stroud), Lloyd (Robert De Niro), Arthur (Clint Kimbrough), and Freddie (Robert Walden). The early postcredit scenes give us an idea of the family life of this group. The setting is the same rural backwoods we saw in the precredit sequence, but instead of the forest, we see the unassuming cabin of the Barkers in the forest. Kate is washing her obviously sexually mature sons, lovingly sponging them down. The father lingers on the sidelines, deferring to Kate to deal with their children as well as the sheriff who comes to accuse Herman, the oldest son, of raping one of the neighbor girls. The contradictions in Kate's value system become quickly apparent when she kisses Herman for admitting to stealing a pie, but slaps one of the other boys for cursing. (This foreshadows the group's—really, Kate's—alternations between murder and religious observance.) She is ruthlessly protective of her children, and equally powerful in her rejection of her husband. She has tremendous ambitions—"You're gonna find me in a palace," she says, a goal that must be achieved by what Robert Warshow called the movie gangster's "drive for success . . . a success that is defined in its most general terms, not as accomplishment or specific gain, but simply as the unlimited possibility of aggression."[8] This concept is crucial in understanding the motivations of the Barkers, with Kate using the concept of "a palace" as a mythological symbol of wealth and attainment that can only be achieved through "unlimited aggression." Because the Barkers do not set limits on themselves—being individual enough to practice incest and rape and later murder on a fairly regular basis—there is little doubt they will achieve "the palace."

This cannot begin to occur, however, until Kate has finally asserted herself by abandoning her husband, her sons' father. "You never could make a decent living . . . you never did mount me proper," she says, a multileveled comment that shows not only Kate's rejection of the static, unambitious, unindividualized, "normal" life-style she sees before her, but also the film's graphic, unsentimentalized approach to sexuality. Kate can leave George Barker because he lacked ambition and left her sexually unsatisfied. Her denial of her husband's place in the family scheme paradoxically binds the group more closely and plants the seeds for the group's destruction, as the film translates their attempts to obtain "a palace" into a mythic search to replace the missing father that Kate has symbolically killed.

As Tom Milne said in *Sight and Sound*, Corman "extends his frame of reference by setting Kate's escape with her sons from the confines of Joplin, Missouri, against newsreel footage of the period. The world in which the Barkers play out their personal drama is one in which Mammon has fallen and God has risen. . . ."[9] The deceptive "documentary" quality noted in *The St. Valentine's Day Massacre* reappears here in the newsreel footage of Mickey Mouse, Aimee Semple McPherson, and the Ku Klux Klan. The real purpose of this footage, how-

ever, is not to create the illusion of *Bloody Mama* as simply a
documentary, but to cast the Barkers' search for success as typical of
the upward mobility celebrated as part of the American way of life.
Just as businessmen are excused from the same kinds of ethics de-
manded of "the man on the street," the Barkers excuse themselves
from such limits, from a life of anonymity, and instead plunge into the
maelstrom of success, using, typically, the most immediate means
available to them to attain it: robbery and murder.

The film's bluntness in showing the sordid details of their life of
crime, their wholehearted rejection of propriety and restraint, is evident during their first bank robbery, when they force a group of old
women to strip to bra and panties and ride on the running board of the
escape car through the city and into the country away from the police.
Ma's noisy upbraiding of these half-naked, silent old women shows how
far removed she is from their way of life. This scene could not have
occurred in the film with which *Bloody Mama* has been most often
compared—Arthur Penn's rosy-eyed *Bonnie and Clyde*. I mention this
not merely to criticize Penn's film but to show how far Corman is willing to go in his ruthless treatment of the material. In the *Sight and
Sound* interview, Corman acknowledged the comparisons to *Bonnie
and Clyde* and said, "my decision was not to romanticize or glorify, but
to stay closer to what I felt the reality was. I had pictures of the Barkers
and I knew what they looked like—they were *not* handsome or pret-
ty."[10] This refusal to glamorize the characters extends to their activities
as well, accounting for much of the force of *Bloody Mama.*

The weak link in the group is hinted at early in the Barkers' crime
career, as Herman attacks and kills a man on a ferry boat. Kate offers
comfort to a crying, overwrought Herman, showing the group's pen-
chant for going through purging rituals to curb any guilt about what
they are doing. Herman is at once the most powerful member of the
group (excepting his mother) and the weakest. He is the most consciously Oedipal of the sons, Ma's most frequent bed partner, and the
one son who seems most obsessed with his father's eyes. During a
jewelry store robbery he resists his natural impulse to kill the clerk
because "He's got eyes like pa's!" Herman's obsession reaches its peak
during the encounters with the kidnap victim, Mr. Pendlebury, who
also has "eyes like Pa."

Aside from their skills with lucratively antisocial activities, none of
the sons fares particularly well outside the enclosed world of Joplin,
Missouri. All of them fall into self-destructive patterns that seem to be
aggravated by Kate. Freddie, the youngest, meets a sadist, Kevin
Dirkman (Bruce Dern), in prison and falls in love with him. Freddie's
fascination with Kevin's brutality is graphically shown as he awaits with
a combination of excitement and terror Kevin's use of his belt. Later,

After Ma Barker (Shelley Winters) abandons her husband, oldest son Herman (Don Stroud) becomes his chief replacement.

Ma sidetracks their relationship by demanding that Kevin sleep with her, an encounter Kevin greets with relish. Freddie reacts by burning himself with a cigarette.

Arthur becomes religion-obsessed, and appears to retreat further from reality as the film progresses. Lloyd becomes a hopeless heroin addict, completely withdrawn from the group in spite of Ma's attempts to rouse him. Herman's crimes land several members of the group in jail; his relationship with the whore Mona (Diane Varsi) is nonexclusive and his brothers all "take their turn." Herman's eventual takeover of the group destroys it.

Ma's intrusions into her sons' lives begin to alienate them. After her senseless killing of the girl Rembrandt, with whom Lloyd had fallen in love, Lloyd has little to do with the group. Her attempts to remove Mona from the group are rebuffed by the only son powerful enough to challenge, and eventually overcome, her—Herman.

The film juxtaposes postcard-beautiful landscapes, particularly lakes and other bodies of water, with the uncontrolled aggression of the Barkers. Their first major crime occurs on a body of water, when Herman and his brothers shake down riders on a ferry boat, then kill one of them. During one of Lloyd's solitary trips to a lake next to one of the gang's hideouts, he meets an engaging, vital swimmer named Rembrandt. After some small talk about her "funny name," Lloyd propositions her. But he adds the caveat: "I take lots of dope." This is probably the most intensely poignant scene in the film, with the proximity of the lake, the vitality and confusion of Rembrandt, and Lloyd's pathetic words, "I'd love to love you . . . ," intermingling. The seriousness of this talk between two strangers translates it into a larger encounter between life and death. His confession of impotence—"You don't have to hit the jackpot every time"—finalizes what is, as David Will has said, "the most illuminating portrait of drug addiction Hollywood has produced." Corman cuts from Rembrandt's struggle to get out of Lloyd's embrace to the same character bound and gagged in the hideout.

Ma's decision to murder Rembrandt because she "may know too much" seems motivated less by a need for efficient management of the group than by her irritation that yet another of her sons is being "led astray" by a woman. It is also the film's most perfect embodiment of Ma's attack on the life-principle, as the vibrant, intense Rembrandt is bound and gagged and incarcerated in their dark house by Ma's order. Ma's jealousy of her sons' involvements is prodigious, and she is eager to kill this threat to her control over them. Corman shoots the death of Rembrandt from underneath the tub of water in which she is being drowned. Corman's use of close-up in this grisly event intensifies the audience's unwilling involvement and complicity in what is happening. We are not so much manipulated to sympathize with Rembrandt, as made to feel somehow part of a world that kills its innocents.

The use of water as a cleansing symbol occurs again in the latter part of the film, when the group finds yet another hideout near a lake. Several elements come together here, including the actual event that brings the police down on the Barkers and the death of Lloyd. The utter brutality of Herman, in particular, is shown when he decides to go alligator-hunting. He uses a live pig as bait, but fires a shotgun to kill the beast, the shots calling attention to him, and tipping off Moses (Scatman Crothers) who in turn calls the police. This event is intercut with shots of Lloyd wandering in the grass near the lake, falling down, and dying from a drug overdose. Again the proximity of the lake transforms a natural formation into a symbol of the preeminence of nature and of what is ironically the most "natural" event in life—death.

Like *Machine Gun Kelly*, *Bloody Mama* prominently features a kidnapping. In both cases this crime simply precipitates the destruction of the gangster group, in the latter case because it aggravates Herman's obsession with his "missing" father and forces him to defy Ma in a way that presages the end. The kidnap victim is Sam Pendlebury (Pat Hingle), a soft-spoken "millionaire," as Ma describes him (he denies this), who is kept in a barn by the group, with his eyes covered over by bandages. The important conversations in these scenes occur between Ma and Pendlebury, and Herman and Pendlebury. The victim admonishes Ma for her "unladylike" behavior, and Ma, in typical response, attempts in vain to seduce him. Herman is annoyed by Pendlebury's frank, easy conversation with him, and is particularly upset when the older man refers to him as "Sonny boy," a too-appropriate nickname for Herman. Pendlebury seems to understand the subtle dynamics of the group and exploits them for his own use by playing the substitute father: "If I was your father, I'd take you over my knees." Ma says to him, "You're a proper, grown-up man, Sam. You're getting to us . . . but we're getting to you, too." In these scenes, which are among the most peaceful in the film, we see the faltering re-creation of the family that was destroyed at the beginning with Ma covering Pendlebury's eyes in her attempt to alter his identity symbolically, to change him into a more acceptable version of her "lost" husband. Herman is particularly hopeful about the possibility of this re-creation, again demanding to see Pendlebury's eyes. "I knew it!" he says. "I think I'm going right out of my mind. *He's got pa's eyes!*" Herman's translation of Sam Pendlebury into his "father" precludes the possibility of following Ma's order and killing him. Instead, the two of them walk into the woods, and Herman fires a few shots into the air. They even shake hands before separating.

Ma's killing of Rembrandt seems to be the point at which the group begins to collapse because, as Corman has pointed out, "Rembrandt's was not a necessary death." But the collapse really began the moment they abandoned Joplin and went into the "real" world. The things that Ma, as an autocrat in her small world, permitted, could not continue indefinitely in society at large. Another, more subtle sign of the group's imminent self-destruction is the departure of Mona. As the hard-core but sensitive whore, Mona was one of only two characters in the film who was able to successfully penetrate the insular world of the Barkers. (The other was Kevin Dirkman, who became one of the sons by sleeping with Ma, yet dies by her hand in the final shootout.) Mona drifts out of their lives with the same world-weary detachment with which she entered.

Already somewhat decimated—having lost Mona, Lloyd, the real father George Barker and the substitute one, Sam Pendlebury—the group retrenches for their final shootout. Corman uses both hand-held and stable camera during this frenzied event, and each of the group meets a violent end. Freddie, in some ways the most childish, innocent of the group, sacrifices himself early by running out of the house into open gunfire. Arthur is shot inside the house. Ma kills Kevin for trying to retreat. Herman, in a successful completion of the motif of eye-obsession, turns the gun on his face and kills himself. Ma's frantic reaction to the destruction of her sons ends with her death.

Corman improvised one aspect of this scene during shooting—the presence of a large group of anonymous picnickers who spread their tablecloths on the grounds surrounding the house. Corman has cited the "realistic" aspect of this conceit, the fact that according to police he spoke with during shooting, many of these shoot-outs tend to have a large audience. A more appropriate explanation for the existence of shots of "normal and typical citizens" enjoying the group's annihilation might lie in Corman's view of a vicious, voyeuristic society no better than the criminals who attempt to break out of it.

4

Experiencing "The Other"

"Paradoxically, when my sight started improving, I began to feel depressed. I often experienced periods of crying. . . . In the evening I preferred to rest in a dark room. Some days I felt confused. I did not know whether to touch or to look. . . . Recovery of sight has been a long and hard road for me, like entering a strange world. In these moments of depression, I sometimes wondered if I was happier before. . . ."[1]

CORMAN'S FILMS EMBODY two distinct but overlapping "worlds." The first is the real world in which his characters move and talk and live. This world appears less frequently than the second, the psychological landscape in which his characters spend their real time. In the Poe films the "second world," the world of "the other," is most obvious because Corman consciously internalizes the action and uses a complex symbology to define the characters, rather than simply "letting them exist." The "plot" occurs either entirely, literally "inside" (*The House of Usher*), or in a combination of inside and artificial, stylized "outside" (*The Premature Burial*). For Corman, the experience of life is radically lopsided. His characters are not dynamic; they cannot change or grow or actualize without submitting entirely to the dangerous world of "the other" (as in the works of Poe himself).

In his schematic breakdown of Corman's films, Paul Willeman describes the movement here as the "effort to escape the eternal cycle."[2] The "cycle" is the birth and death of culture, of the individual, the movement from an inchoate condition of philosophical and psychological ignorance, to consciousness, to death. Stripped of all trappings, the cycle leads inevitably to death.

The "other" provides the unactualized personality with the hope of liberation from this cycle, by replacing the dull, hopeless world of "reality" with one that draws its whole existence from that personality's fears, dreams, and desires. The elaborate color design of the Poe films, *The Trip*, and *X—The Man with the X-Ray Eyes*, fleshes out the mental landscapes of suffering characters like Roderick Usher, Paul Groves,

Peter Fonda as Paul Groves experiences "death" in The Trip.

69

and Dr. Xavier. Even Xavier's name is mysterious—the "X" *is* "the
other."

The spiritual world, the sense of "otherness," experienced by Paul
Groves and Dr. Xavier comes from the same kind of personality, the
hypersensitive "artist" (Paul makes commercials, Xavier is a brilliant
surgeon and experimental chemist), and their "worlds" are in many
ways similar. Both hunger for enlightenment and are willing to compromise their social standing (particularly Xavier, who sees his own
prestige as a shackling force), in order to attain special self-knowledge.
Both men depart on a journey (a literal "trip" in both cases) with all
the signs of the classic heroic quest for self seen in myth and legend.
Dr. Xavier passes through a variety of incarnations after his encounter
with his own "mystical" powers of sight, including working in one of
the most mythologically resonant environments, a carnival, like Willeman's view of the playground in *The Intruder*, a "safety valve for society's repressed instincts." Paul, too, changes in *The Trip*. We see him
in his own fantasies as alternatively bound, passive, and aggressive,
questioning, indicating the warring factions of the intelligent, but
unenlightened personality.

The "other" appears in various forms in the films, most clearly as
the whole spiritual world to which the hero subjects himself in the
search for meaning, an action triggered by some distinctly antisocial,
antistatus quo action (Paul Groves drops acid; Dr. Xavier "accidentally"
kills one of his best friends). More specifically, "the other" appears as
various incarnations of the personality whose world this is, particularly
as the "anima" of Jungian psychology (both Glenn and Sally in *The
Trip*). The anima can express the searching character's simultaneous
hope for liberation and need for destruction.

The chief characteristic of the world of "the other" is, in Jungian
parlance, "the return of the repressed," the character's own desire for
destruction, chaos, and collapse that lurks beneath a socially adjusted,
"successful" exterior. *The Trip* and *X—The Man with the X-Ray Eyes*
represent two slightly different approaches to the same question, with
Paul Groves's ultimately life-affirming experience with "the other"
countered by Dr. Xavier's self-destruction as he drifts continuously
away from an ordered life into the mysteries of his own personality.

The Trip

Corman expands some concerns expressed in his previous film, *The
Wild Angels*, in his major drug film, *The Trip* (1967). Like its predecessor, *The Trip* focuses on an outlaw group within society, but it ex-
amines this group with greater intensity than *The Wild Angels*, and
couples the violent rejection of a moribund society by its youth with

an archetypal search for identity on the part of its main character, Paul Groves. The material vandalism of the gang members of *The Wild Angels* or *Teenage Doll* (ten years earlier) evolves into the ultimate form of juvenile deliquency in *The Trip*—the creation of a youth culture that stubbornly violates convention, the turning by youth to themselves alone and the consequent refusal to even acknowledge the existence of parental/patriarchal/authoritarian structures by this group no longer interested in maintaining the status quo.

Corman opens the scene with what appears to be a simple criticism of American consumer society. We hear distinctly period music—a downbeat theme by the Electric Flag, a well-known psychedelic blues group from the period—and the counterpointing image shows an elegantly dressed couple embracing while a voiceover intones: "With April in Paris, anything is possible." The camera then zooms back to show that the couple appear to be standing on water. This mock-religious image merges a seemingly spiritual occurrence with the false values of the advertising/filmmaking world. (The scene is a commercial being shot by Paul.) This immediately suggests both the artificiality of Paul's world and the failure of religion to provide any answers, since it is simply being employed as a merchandising tool. The phrase "anything is possible" takes on ironic meaning as the film documents the arid, impossible existence of its principal character.

Who is Paul Groves? Like Walter Paisley in *Bucket of Blood* or any of the Poe heroes, he bears a resemblance to Corman that cannot be ignored. Both are seen as highly intelligent "artists" working in crassly commercial circumstances. Both work in a visual medium—hence both are concerned with "seeing," enlightenment. Both belittle their "job"—Paul says, "What else can I do? I've got to make a living." Like Paul, Corman took LSD and spoke about his experiences at length. Paul is a burned-out character—like Corman, a "traveler in two worlds." The first is the world of business and finance and "false creativity"—providing fanciful, hollow commercial images that society can use to validate its existence ("With April in Paris"—that is, with the ultimate superficial smothering of man's "basic" animal nature—"anything is possible"). The second is the world of self-absorption and self-discovery, the world of the "trip," of the turning away from the empty comfort of social structures into the mysterious realm of the self. Paul's sense of alienation necessitates the trip: "I think I'll find out something about myself."

The failure of such a civilized institution as marriage is shown during the scene that immediately follows the "April in Paris" segment, when Paul's estranged wife, Sally (Susan Strasberg), arrives on the "set" (a cliff above the mythically resonant ocean), angry that Paul has missed his appointment with the lawyers. Corman shoots their encounter with tactful economy, relying on the expressions of the actors to show the supreme difficulty of relationships as well as marriage, as they quietly argue about Paul's negligence. They must argue quietly because they are both highly "civilized" people—unable to commit the "sin" of violent emotional response. Intensity is not an element in Paul's character; he reacts to his wife's irritation by apologizing. She realizes the gulf between them—symbolized here by the vast ocean—and gives him a quick, bitter kiss on the cheek before she leaves.

The film shows Paul's entry into a more mythic, less structured world when he enters a garishly furnished and painted "hippie" club with the intention of taking LSD. The sets appear gushingly self-expressive and disorderly—the world "Love" is painted in huge letters across the sidewalk—signaling his abandonment of the orderly, empty structures of his life (his job, failing marriage). The heavily controlling director we saw during the opening gives way to a more questioning, naive, dependent personality: handed a black mask by his mentor in the trip, John (Bruce Dern), he asks, "Should I put it on?" Divorced from his normal life, Paul does not quite know how to proceed, "what to do."

He surrounds himself with cultural artifacts—a kind of safety valve in reminding him if the trip becomes "too much" (i.e., the burden of self-discovery, identity, becomes overwhelming) that culture, society, civilization still exist and will welcome his return. John contradicts this idea when he tells Paul to "let everything run out of you," that is, to erase or dissolve the stagnant personality and allow for the entry of a new, more enlightened and satisfied one. Paul's desperate desire for this enlightenment helps him "put on the mask" literally and figuratively—erasing what he "sees" in the real world and allowing him to explore what is "inside."

The images of these initial stages of the trip vacillate between life-affirming and life-denying. The orderly world becomes a nonsense pattern of kaleidoscopic imagery that scrambles his perception of reality, intercut with scenes of isolation in nature (he runs alone over rocks by the sea) and entrapment/entombment (he is chained to a wall). His experience makes him feel that "everything's alive"—as opposed to his normal dead existence.

Paul's friend John emerges during these early scenes as a complex character—a mythical "opener of the way" to the hero's classic quest for integration or identity, but one who is himself already "aware," and exhibits more concern for Paul, almost fear of what enlightenment can bring, than mere camaraderie or pleasure in his friend simply "getting high."

The film intercuts continuously between exterior views of Paul and his experience, and illustrations of what he is seeing and feeling. His reversion to childhood, to innocence, to the "clean slate" of an un-molded personality, is shown during his immersion in a peculiar in-house pool that extends between two rooms, one of the film's many symbols of Paul's divided consciousness and the need to undergo purg-ing rituals to achieve the self.

During the early segments of the trip, Paul recasts his poor relations with Sally into a near-mystical fantasy of sexual, philosophical, and spiritual communion. Their initial bitter encounter in the wide, empty space of nature reappears during the trip as a Dionysian ritual of love-making, their naked bodies intertwined amid flashing lights and psy-chedelic imagery. During this scene he articulates his inability to know: "It's true that I love her. But I don't know what that means, for which I'll suffer. I don't want to suffer." Paul's fear of "suffering" be-comes clearer as the trip progresses—"suffering" is a metaphor for death.

As Paul's experience continues and expands, the images become stronger and more negative. These scenes introduce one of the film's major motifs: running. Paul is shown constantly running, escaping, an apt metaphor in a film concerned with the double movement toward self-actualization and self-destruction. Corman cross-cuts here be-tween two important scenes: Paul running in long shot across an empty beach, an image of both dehumanization (since he is engulfed by na-ture) and the positive reassertion of nature over the quirks of human personality (he is "at one with" nature, not suffering); and walking in medium-shot to closeup through the dark environment of one of Cor-man's own Poe films. Even as he is experiencing a sort of rapture, at peace with nature in the sand, another side of his personality is expe-riencing death: he sees himself hanging in the Poe chamber. A com-plementary image shows Paul bound to a chair by the monklike figures from *Masque of the Red Death* or *The Pit and the Pendulum*, who cover him completely and lay a mask over his face. This sinking of personality deep into the physical body marks Paul's new awareness, even experiencing, of death. When Corman cuts from these trip im-ages to a more objective shot of Paul, we see him swimming naked—without defenses—in the inside pool. His next words crystallize what he is learning: "Oh no, oh no, I'm not gonna die . . . I'm gonna die! I want out, man! I don't want to die!" Corman reinforces Paul's weakness with a high angle shot. The use of the Poe motifs in the sequence leading up to this further validates the Paul Groves–Corman connec-tion, as the things Paul "experiences" are images that demonstrably come out of his mind, but that actually came out of Corman's mind since they are lifted from the director's own Poe films.

Paul's "progress" is attended by various figures along the way, who take on mythic proportions as part of the mythic nature of Paul's search. John in particular solidifies his role as the "wise man" who has already experienced what Paul is feeling. When Paul reveals his agitating fear of death, John replies, "If that happens to you again, you go ahead and go with it. Just go ahead and die." That is, yield to the experience of death in order to be reborn stronger. Another character who appears at key points of Paul's trip is Glenn (Salli Sachse), a beautiful blonde who appears within his fantasies, and as a detached but interested, almost anthropological observer from outside. She appears initially as the hoped-for reward for Paul's attempt to find enlightenment, reappears mysteriously during the final trip sequence in the club, and again at the end, when he "attains" her and shares with her "what he has learned."

The film stresses the innocent nature of Paul Groves throughout, even while it advances a view of the character as "guilty." During one of the trip sequences, he enters a fantasy-playground in which Max (Dennis Hopper) dissects his personality in the manner of a prosecutor. Max's final judgment of Paul's "crime" is that of "no real love and total self-absorption," to which Paul admits, "I'm guilty." But he is not guilty, or not viewed as such; Corman demonstrates his innocence, his frailty, his openness to the possibility of self-realization in a variety of ways. The most important of these is in Paul's rejection of character-veiling devices such as sarcasm and verbal paradox. When he realizes the inherent paradox of the phrase "living room," he reacts angrily at John's amusement at his discovery. During his encounter with the woman in the laundromat (Barboura Morris), he asks her a simple, if redundant question: "Are you doing your wash?" When she replies, "No, I come in here every night to dine," he expresses confusion and irritation at her sarcasm: "Why do you say things like that?" Paul's sense of honesty reaches her, and when she decides to talk more directly to him, he notices this and reacts with pleasurable interest: "You're changing now. That's nice."

Another way in which Corman validates the view of the innocent in a confused, corrupt world is during the scene where Paul breaks into a sterile middle-class home to watch television. Significantly, the picture on the television is entirely blurred, but the audio is an acerbic newsman voice talking about what happened in Vietnam that day. A child appears on a landing above him, and they engage in the following conversation:

GIRL: Who are you?
PAUL: I'm just a man.
GIRL: What do you want?
PAUL: I'm resting. Okay?

GIRL: I want some milk.

PAUL: All right. Let's go get it.

The girl is without fear, not having reached this point in her civilized progress, and she takes his hand and leads him to the kitchen. The simple directness of the conversation, the instant ease and rapport between two strangers, one a child and one a man perhaps equally "unevolved," searching, aligns the two characters as variations of the same kind of personality. The conversation continues:

GIRL: Where's my daddy?

PAUL: He's upstairs asleep. Shall we go sit down?

GIRL: Okay. (He leads her along.)

PAUL: Okay.

GIRL: I'm sleepy now.

PAUL: You better go back up. Do you want me to take you?

GIRL: Where will you sleep?

PAUL: I don't know.

GIRL: What's your name?

PAUL: Paul.

At this point the father appears and demands to know who Paul is, and what he is doing there. It is significant that the film's most successful merging of two personalities should be between two seemingly opposed types: a little girl, and a grown man. It is also important that this connection is broken at the point at which the girl asks Paul to identify himself. The father appears immediately after Paul says his name, and Paul flees, that is, at the precise moment when the burden of identity, of "who I am," reappears. This quiet scene of ordinary human communion precedes yet another of Paul's trip experiences, another plunge into the "search."

This scene bears a strong resemblance to what is probably the most famous sequence in the film, the seriocomic encounter in a laundromat between an ordinary citizen, a woman in curlers washing her laundry on a Friday night, and Paul Groves. The scene contains many telling elements, including Paul's fascination with the mundane (of a washing machine in motion he says: "it's incredible!"), his reinvesting of ordinary life with a feeling of meaning; his attempt to "really communicate," as he tells the woman, by expressing honest feeling and avoiding sarcasm and verbal play; his desire to "get out," to escape, again given a precise visual analogue in his stopping a spinning dryer and throwing out—liberating!—the woman's sheets onto the floor. This latter scene also shows how the film uses humor as a deflation for the seriousness of Paul's search, as he says of her clothes, "We've got to get them out of there!"

During the last major trip sequence in the club, we see the same kinds of "juvenile delinquents" visible in earlier Corman movies, engaging here in wild dancing that self-consciously recalls pagan rituals. This group has abandoned the social superstructure in favor of the experiential, the rejection of duty, regularity, and conformity in the altering of consciousness through drugs, in the hedonistic revelry that characterizes the club, and the use of "pagan" visual icons such as body painting, bizarre clothes, and light shows. The film incorporates only one representative of the "real world," the police, but it treats them with the same sense of fantasy as the trip images; indeed, we see the police moving through a crowd at the club in the same way we see the crowded characters in the trip sequences, as simply one element in a larger tableau. They work as a fear-element, much like the Poe-executioner character earlier, but are hardly dwelt on or defined. During Paul's meeting with Glenn at the club, she sums up the irrelevance of the police and all they represent: "What police? There *are* no police. I don't *believe* in police." Her success at living in the unstructured world of the "youth cult" is not mirrored in Paul, who expresses paranoid fear of the police.

The Trip leaves open the question of what Paul has learned; this was Corman's intent. Unlike classic myth patterns, where a "search" must end in a resolution, Paul's experience is treated with typical Corman detachment. After he "comes down," he makes love to Glenn, and they exchange the following words:

GLENN: Did you find what you were looking for? The insight?

PAUL: Yeah. I think—like, I *love* you.

GLENN: And everybody else.

PAUL: Yeah. And everybody else.

GLENN: It's easy now. Wait till tomorrow.

PAUL: Yeah? Well, I'll think about that tomorrow.

This is a conversation by turns cynical (Glenn) and open-ended (Paul). Corman shoots the scene with Glenn entirely off-screen, so that she assumes the role of a "voice" within Paul, a part of him that realizes that he may have gained nothing by the trip, that human nature cannot change. Paul's conscious feeling is a little more hopeful, as he turns Glenn's use of the negative "tomorrow" (perhaps inability to maintain a relationship) into something he will deal with later.

The famous orgy from the church in The Wild Angels *(1966)—Peter Fonda, standing center.*

AIP did not approve of *The Trip*, though there is evidence they approved of the film's commercial success. Judith Crist referred to it as "a one-and-one-half-hour commercial for LSD," and AIP echoed this sentiment by attaching bookend disclaimers. The opening precredit screen has a written narration warning of "dire consequences" for those who use LSD; and the freeze-frame image of Paul that ends the film is marred by a cracked-glass image the studio superimposed, to make it clear that even if Corman seemed to endorse the drug, they felt it was simply dangerous and wanted to discourage its use. Corman's success with the film supersedes these clumsy intrusions; and it is a tribute to the intensity of his vision that the drug should simply be a triggering device, unimportant in itself, in one character's search for self.

X—The Man with the X-Ray Eyes

During the mid-1950s, Corman directed as many as eight films a year (1956)—in addition to producing for other directors. After 1960 his output began to decrease, until by the late 1960s he was averaging

one film every two years. One of the last of Corman's frantically pro-
ductive years was 1963, and as in the early days the films are about
equally divided between disengaged minor and finished major works.
The energy Corman put into *Attack of the Crab Monsters* or *It Conquered the World*, both 1956, for example, counterpoints the relative
lifelessness of *She Gods of Shark Reef* or *Naked Paradise* the same
year. Four of his five films for 1963 can be divided equally into failures
(*The Young Racers, The Terror*) and successes (*The Raven, The Haunted Palace*), but the other film from that year, *X—The Man with the X-
Ray Eyes*, ranks above even his successes for that year in its grim embodiment of Corman's nihilistic worldview. Corman was blessed with
an exceptional script by Robert Dillon and Ray Russell, taken from a
short story by Russell. His other important collaborators—Daniel
Haller and Floyd Crosby—also contribute a great deal to one of Corman's most striking films.

The graphic nature of the film is signaled by the precredit sequence,
which consists of two shots. The first is a closeup of what appears to be
a huge eyeball against a red background. The camera simply lingers
on this image, for an inordinate amount of time, without moving or
cutting. Finally there is a cut to the same eye floating in a jar of gaseous
liquid—again a detached image, simply thrust at the audience, with
no background to distract us from it. The film's obsession with eyes
and "seeing" is previewed, but the gruesomeness of the detached eyeball hints at the negative meaning of "sight" that underlies the film.

The first shot after the credits shows another eye closeup, but this
time it is part of a living human being. Dr. James Xavier (Ray Milland).
He is being examined by his friend, Dr. Sam Brant (Harold J. Stone).
Brant is mystified by being asked to examine Xavier's eyes again after
having done so only three months earlier. It seems Xavier is doing
experiments with "vision." Dissatisfied with the abject ignorance of
mankind as symbolized by the fact that the human eye sees "only one-
tenth of the actual wave spectrum," Xavier is concocting an experimental serum that will expand human vision. He expresses his motivation in both lofty and practical terms: increased sight could help man
probe "the mysteries of creation" and give him "power to learn, to
create, to *do*"; in the hospital setting that comprises much of Xavier's
world it would have practical value in allowing doctors to make absolutely true diagnoses, with no guesswork.

Xavier does have to explain his motivations, since he is beholden for
experiment money to a "foundation" that finances such projects. Another friend, Dr. Diane Fairfax (Diane Van der Vlis), acts as a liaison
between Xavier and the foundation to procure him money. The film
shows the utter seriousness of Xavier's experiments to himself and his

impatience at having to deal with the foundation at all. It also demonstrates his ability to assume a godlike control. When Sam Brant complains that his experiments are intruding on the territory of "the gods," Xavier articulates an unmistakable hubris by remarking sardonically, "My dear doctor, I am closing in on the gods." During the development of the serum, he injects a small amount into the eyes of a laboratory monkey. The monkey lives long enough only to show that the serum indeed works. In a scene that summarizes Corman's view of the position of mankind at the mercy of a malevolent Creator, the camera lingers on the caged monkey as it lies on its back and dies. Xavier is unconcerned.

His experiments have increased his vision to the point where he can see inside people's bodies, determining exactly what is wrong with them. Dr. Willard Benson (John Hoyt), an "important" doctor, is planning an operation on a young girl based on what Xavier discovers is a wrong diagnosis. His pleading with Benson to reconsider his diagnosis does not sway the doctor, and Xavier is forced to take over the operation after it has begun. Benson's refusal to consider Xavier's "facts" can be seen as an indication of a patriarchal stubbornness in a dying culture. What Xavier is fighting is the world around him, a world particularly populated by people like Benson—refined, intelligent, but cold, unfeeling functionaries. This view is supported by the presence of the "foundation," all old men, whose narrow-minded attitudes determine whether Xavier will be allowed to continue his experiments. Xavier actively attacks this world at the point at which he slashes Dr. Benson's hand to disable him from operating. This is Xavier's initial break from the normal routine of his stagnating world, an attack on patriarchy represented by Benson.

The film uses the dead monkey as a melodramatic foreshadowing of Xavier's own fate. The creature's ability to "see" more deeply into things is followed quickly by its death, as if "sight," a metaphor for understanding, enlightenment, must trigger self-destruction. Xavier typically blames the monkey's death on its inability "to comprehend or adjust to what it saw, or saw through." The implication is that he, on the other hand, will be able to "comprehend" and "adjust." His first use of the serum is attended by Sam, whom he persuades to help him. His jubilation at being able to read one paper through another is followed by a traumatic reaction to the second administering. Like the monkey, he cannot comprehend or adjust; he screams at whatever he has seen, and Corman fades the scene. We learn that he has been "unconscious." This brief comatose state is a kind of death and rebirth for Xavier, who awakens with new determination to enter a different world that will offer him superior insight and intelligence.

The film breaks the tension of Xavier's obsessiveness by inserting a scene where he attends a party at which he sees beneath everyone's clothes as they dance. The scene is treated with high humor, as Xavier indulges in an ironic interchange with a flirtatious woman who says, "I like the way you look . . . urgent." Even here, however, the theme of seeing appears, though in a comic context. She insists she saw him "all the way across the room" and he compliments her on her "sharp eyes." It is significant that this scene appears early. Shot with discreetly covered naked bodies, the scene is reminiscent of the dancing teenagers from AIP's beach films popular at the time. The film contains virtually no humor from this point on, as Dr. Xavier's world changes drastically.

Xavier's consuming desire to "see" more and more begins to estrange him from his peers. The foundation withdraws its support after it hears a tape of his first self-experiment with the drug, which ends with Xavier screaming. After Xavier's takeover of Dr. Benson's operation, Benson tells him that, significantly, "I don't know what I saw," but says he will charge him with malpractice. The final break for Xavier occurs when he "accidentally" kills his friend, Sam. This is an especially troubling occurrence since it follows Xavier telling Sam that he will continue his experiments and that "I want you to be with me, Sam." Sam's worry about his friend causes him to approach him with a sedative-filled hypodermic, and Xavier flings his arm up to avoid the injection, accidentally knocking Sam through the window behind them.

Corman visualizes the transition of Xavier from the stiff, orderly world of the hospital into the chaos of "enlightenment" in an extraordinary montage. This is preceded by Diane talking to him, turning, and seeing he is not there. He is racing down a back staircase, Corman alternating head and feet shots and superimposing newspaper headlines tracing the development of the case. The dizzying movements in the montage show Xavier's breakthrough into another world. This world is shown in the shot immediately following the montage—another dizzying movement following the arc of a ferris wheel, the camera moving epically down as the giant machine moves. It is significant that Xavier's next world should be a carnival—a place where normal routines and activities are suspended in favor of "fun." The carnival is a metaphysical landscape populated by magicians and spiritualists and—except for Dr. Xavier—charlatans. It is a place where "anything can happen."

Xavier forms an uneasy alliance with a hard-boiled shyster, Crane (Don Rickles), who has given him a new identity as "Mentalo," a mindreader. Xavier's passage into a mystical world is shown by the outrageous costume he wears—gaudy spiritualist robes and, most disturbingly, a white cloth across his eyes on which is painted one large eye. Xavier is like a fallen god, an idol possessing great powers but utterly victimized by them. The same supernatural talent that provides "answers" for others merely creates new questions for Xavier.

Earlier Xavier has expressed his desire to learn "the mysteries of creation," but during his first appearance as Mentalo we see what he really learns. After doing several typical "tricks" of analyzing the contents of various pockets, Mentalo-Xavier addresses a young man (Dick Miller) who claims he is a fake. The disturbing-amusing tone of the early part of this scene becomes merely disturbing as Mentalo describes his questioner. After telling him his name and hometown and Social Security number, he says, "You also have a letter in your pocket from a girl you deserted." Xavier's truths are sordid ones: the reality of human misery and alienation in this scene are followed by the reality of disease and death during Mentalo's next incarnation as "The Healer."

The preeminence of Xavier's extraordinary eyes over his mind and body is shown in his increasingly bizarre appearance. As Mentalo, he presents an image of mystical resonance, his business suit replaced by colorful, outré robes and his real eyes covered by a cloth on which a false, third eye is painted, that is, his human consciousness hidden by the superhuman one. Like Paul Johnson in *Not of this Earth*, Xavier wears extremely dark glasses when he is not dressed as Mentalo. Later he replaces these with larger, darker, thicker ones, divorcing himself further from normalcy and humanity.

An outcast from the world of hospitals and doctors and healing, Xavier becomes an outcast even among the carnival people with whom he works. During a conversation at which he is absent, one of them says, "People run from his show" because he "sees too much" and they dislike what they hear. When Xavier intrudes on them and asks what they would do with the power he has, they reveal again the pettiness of human motive: one man says he would have "a hold on people" and make people do things "my way." Another suggests he should "help people from hurting each other," but the idea is framed in a joke. Crane suggests he would look at "all the undressed women my poor eyes could stand." Xavier has gained insights from his experiences, but they are negative, and unpleasant. He sees "ideas, thoughts, differences" as separating people, with no possibility of bringing them together. His tragedy is shown when he speaks wistfully about being "a man" and "being able to open my eyes."

Xavier is not the only character in the film concerned with "seeing," discovering the "truth." Earlier, Dr. Benson said, "I don't know what I saw," but his position in the scheme of the film shows him incapable of seeing. Crane spends a great deal of time trying to comprehend the mystery of Xavier, and Corman at one point shows Xavier continuing his experiments in the sordid storefront the two have rented but the camera moves away from Xavier toward a grimy window through which Crane watches. Regulating what they "see" becomes for these characters a way to maintain or achieve position, status, money—all false values in the scheme of the film. During Xavier's ill-fated trip to Las Vegas, the owner is concerned about Xavier's ability to "see," not surprising considering the latter's bizarre appearance.

The film treats Xavier as a complex mixture of motives—pride and compassion, arrogance and sympathy. During the Las Vegas sequence, just after closing a table, he recklessly demonstrates his powers to onlookers by naming undrawn cards. In spite of the frightening effects of the serum—shown during several scenes where Corman shows Xavier administering the drops, pausing then screaming, followed by a fade—Xavier continues to use it, pushing himself, until he can no longer sleep, since he can see through his own eyelids. Yet Xavier's human side emerges throughout. His salvation of the little girl in the hospital contradicted hospital rules, but it combined Xavier's great powers of sympathy with his desire to "close in on the gods." During his last days at the carnival, he risks exposure as Dr. James Xavier by analyzing the injuries of a girl who has fallen from one of the carnival rides. Corman shoots this scene with a typical crane shot moving slowly forward but stopping short above the characters.

Corman has complained about his lack of budget for the special effects, but the use of "Spectarama"—merely a name for tinted color and negative reversals—is effective because of the way it is framed. Corman uses special effects to show what Xavier sees—"limbs without flesh, girders without steel." These scenes are point of view shots of Xavier's "other world" beneath the surface of people, objects, and buildings, and they are always shown framed within a circle that represents the human pupil, a formal device that supports the film's themes.

Xavier's progress throughout the film is marked by passages from one distinct world into another. First it is the world of his professional, surface life—the hospital. A frantic montage brings us into his second world and a new identity—Mentalo in the carnival. The restless Xavier assumes a third identity, again with the help of the leechlike Crane, as "The Healer," an ironic amplification of Xavier's obvious inability to heal himself. Passing from the magical world of the carnival into a filthy basement apartment in the slums, Crane exploits "The Healer," by luring the poor, aged, sick, and dying for "consultations" to reveal their problems. His first case is a resounding success. He tells an old woman worried about "the cancer" that "it's nothing . . . just tiredness, and age, and nothing." Xavier's emphasis on "nothing" is more than a medical diagnosis at this point; it indicates the quality of his existence.

Corman treats this period in Xavier's life in a montage-heavy sequence that alternates tracking shots toward the startling image of "The Healer" in gogglelike dark glasses with similar tracks toward his wretched customers. He continues to use what is left of the serum and the traumatic nature of his insights is shown in a high-angle shot of Xavier lying in bed in his little apartment behind his "healing room." He tries to sleep, opening and closing his eyes, sees through the floors above him and screams.

Dr. Xavier had not found satisfaction in his associates at the beginning of the film. The other doctors represented for the most part men of limited imagination in a pitifully limited, sterile environment. But what kind of people comprise his world after the experiments? They are characterized by a feeling of hopelessness, of sickness real or imagined. As "The Healer" Xavier treats far more people than he could have as a legal doctor, and the role takes on a double irony since it is the same kind of job he had before, except that now he cannot act on what he knows by treating them, he can "only look," as he says. His insight is that mankind is abjectly ignorant and miserable, alienated and fearful of death. This insight leaves him powerless to act, except, as we see, against himself.

Xavier breaks his bond with Crane after Diane Fairfax discovers him working in the dingy basement. Significantly, he does not recognize her when she comes in. Even after she talks to him, he does not know her. He cannot see *her* anymore, only what is within her. Even after she identifies herself, he questions her. She says simply, "I'm here now," and he replies, "If what I'm seeing is really you." He is far beyond the stage of normal human recognition. He articulates his dilemma: "I'd give anything—anything!—to have dark." During their trip to Las Vegas—where he hopes to use his powers to get enough money to discover a "cure" for his condition—Xavier gives a speech in the spirit of those speeches in the Poe films that define the peculiar world in which their protagonists live. Xavier sees "the city as if it were unborn . . . limbs without flesh . . . steel without girders . . . the city of the dead. . . ."

Las Vegas represents the fourth world into which Xavier passes, a world, like the carnival, dominated by bright colors and the suspension of "normal" activities. The mythic nature of the environment, however, is belied by the quality of frenzy and desperation we see during the last scene here. When Xavier wins $20,000 by using his eyes to identify cards, he arouses the suspicion of the club owner. Xavier's arrogance takes over and he flaunts his godlike ability to penetrate the cards, identifying them before they are drawn. When he tries to cash in his chips, his protective glasses are accidentally removed and his eyes revealed. This is our first true sight of Xavier as he has changed.

The secret of Dr. Xavier (Ray Milland) revealed in X—The Man with the X-Ray Eyes. *Courtesy of American International.*

His eyes are jet black, with only a hint of a pupil. His hysterical reaction to the light further marks him, as the onlookers recoil. The club owner's threat to call the sheriff is answered by Xavier throwing his $20,000 into the crowd, which dives onto the money. This creates enough of a disturbance to allow Xavier to flee, but without Diane. His abandonment of Diane at this point marks his final passage from hope into utter nihilism.

Corman uses a mixture of high overhead shots of Xavier's car careening down the highway through the desert and closeups of the frantic Xavier without his glasses. His hysteria is seen in the wide movements from one side of the highway to the other, oblivious of other drivers as he uses sheer movement to escape the horror of seeing. Xavier's incipient self-destruction is marked by the presence of a helicopter—a frequent symbol of godlike power in films—whose driver tells him, "You can't escape . . . there is no hope . . . all roads are blocked," a speech significantly couched in philosophical as much as practical terms.

Whereas the earlier worlds in which Xavier found himself were at least filled with people—however pitiful or unpleasant—his fifth and final world is the bleak openness of the desert. Just as he suffers symbolic death throughout the film as his sight becomes unbearably powerful, he drives off the highway and crashes, yet does not die. During this final sequence the film shows itself conclusively as a religious parable. Xavier's encounter with a desert evangelist and his flock is shot as a wholly artificial, nonrealistic happening. Xavier's desperation is clear as he staggers toward the tent, toward potential salvation. But the parishioners appear to be almost choreographed in their responses to the preacher's proddings, a wonderfully exact symbol of the enslavement of ignorant mankind by a callous God. This nonnatural behavior by the puppetlike parishioners is counterpointed by Xavier's combination of suffering and his unrelenting need to understand and to "tell others." Asked if he wants salvation, he emphatically recoils: "No!" Instead, "I want to tell you what I see. There are great darknesses, farther than time itself . . . and in the center of the universe, the eye that sees us all! No!" Xavier's hubris is recognized as such by the preacher, who presents a malign image, furthered by his suggestion to Xavier—and seconded by the parishioners—that he follow the Bible's proscription: "If thine eye offend thee, pluck it out." The final shot of the film follows the chants of the others to "pluck it out! pluck it out!" Xavier shows a certain relief as he realizes this is an answer, a way out of his problem. He tears his eyes out. In the film's final shot, Corman shows briefly the anguished face of Xavier without eyes.

X—The Man with the X-Ray Eyes works out Corman's nihilistic worldview with more thoroughness than any of his other films. While

Corman is decidedly antiromantic (with rare exceptions such as *Masque of the Red Death*), *X—Man with the X-Ray Eyes* goes farther than his other films in showing a world dominated by a cruel God who punishes any who challenge Him by burdening them with "insight" and exacting a sacrifice in the form of self-mutilation. The film attacks both the philosophical status quo and the whole concept of patriarchy, represented in characters like Dr. Benson and the "foundation" that directs certain aspects of Xavier's life. The film is also the clearest expression of Corman's customary reversal of the liberal humanist cliché that "Knowledge is power." Understanding, comprehension— symbolized by the ability to "see"—triggers individual destruction, since the "discovery," the enlightenment that dissatisfied characters like Dr. Xavier or Tom Anderson (*It Conquered the World*) or Prince Prospero (*Masque of the Red Death*) achieve is the realization that life is a pointless charade, characterized by sickness and misery and the mysterious, inevitable movement toward the grave.

The film received mostly positive reviews, even from the entrenched bourgeois press represented by the *New York Times*. In spite of its award for best entry in the 1963 Trieste Science Fiction Festival, the film is a complex yet ruthlessly single-minded investigation of the nature of reality. The only "science fiction" aspect of the story is its use of what is really a simple dramatic element—the experimental drug that allows Dr. Xavier to increase his optical sensitivity. Corman's willingness to follow the story to the farthest extremes without flinching— including Xavier ripping out his own eyes—takes the film far beyond its formulaic origins.

5

Corman and Poe

"There is another world, but it is in this one. . . ."

—Paul Eluard

"Reality is another name for death."

—James Purdy, *The House of
the Solitary Maggot*

"She was too aware. . . ."

—Nicholas Medina in *The Pit
and the Pendulum*

THE POE SERIES REPRESENTS Corman's greatest single achievement. "Single" is not in this case inappropriate in describing the six films discussed here,[1] since they contain enough formal and thematic similarities to be considered six variations on the same story. The endlessly recurring images and icons from *The Fall of the House of Usher* (1960) to *The Tomb of Ligeia* (1964), far from merely echoing each other, combine to give substance to one of the most meticulously detailed, self-consciously symbolic yet utterly credible worlds in the history of the cinema.

House of Usher evolved out of Corman's frustration at being asked again by AIP to shoot two black and white exploitation films. He proposed instead to make one color film, offering the Poe project as a possibility. Corman's was not the first Poe film, but previous attempts seemed colorless and unimaginative by contrast, from Robert Florey's 1932 *Murders in the Rue Morgue* to Roy del Ruth's 1954 remake, the 3-D *Phantom of the Rue Morgue*. It should not surprise us that the most frequently filmed Poe stories should be his whodunits, since the formulaic, gamelike nature of this genre translates easily to film.

Two aspects of Poe's work have defeated most filmmakers: the brevity of most of his stories, and their utter lack of realistic "characters" or "action." When he subtitled his story "Shadow" with the phrase "A

Vincent Price as Verden Fell in Tomb of Ligeia.

Parable," Poe was accurately describing the bulk of his work, wherein mood is the chief element and even landscapes and houses exist primarily as analogues for the unbalanced human mind. The difficulties posed by his work seemed insurmountable, in spite of the fact that Poe's fiction and poetry are in the public domain, a fact hardly lost on Corman.

The gulf between such typical AIP films as Gene Fowler's *I Was a Teenage Werewolf* or Corman's own *Machine Gun Kelly* and a project like *The Fall of the House of Usher* appears extreme. Certainly, the Poe project initiated a new period for both Corman and AIP, with color replacing black and white, ambitious projects preempting the earlier straightforward genre efforts, shooting schedules doubled and tripled, and budgets increased. AIP's stock company, actors like Jonathan Haze and Dick Miller, fell into occasional, minor roles in films fronted by more "serious" and better-known actors including Vincent Price and Boris Karloff. This was true even in the non-Corman post-1960 AIP films, including the topical-satirical beach films.

Poe found a surprisingly sympathetic collaborator in Corman, not only because of a shared fascination with abnormal psychology and the repression of the self, but because Corman too usually emphasized ambience at the expense of action. In Corman's films, "atmosphere" defines the world as it exists for his characters (*The Undead, A Bucket of Blood*). Action is something normally beyond the capability of Corman's characters, particularly the men, who appear obsessed with "meaning" and whose attempts to discover some sense of meaning or identity usually ends in literal or symbolic death at the hands of a grasping female (*Machine Gun Kelly, House of Usher*) or by self-destruction (*X—Man with the X-Ray Eyes, Masque of the Red Death*).

The world of Corman's Poe films, from *House of Usher*, which established the model for the entire series, is dominated by the double fear of sexuality and death. Sexuality is usually represented by a woman with a strong, sensual personality whose needs remain unsatisfied by her more metaphysically inclined husband. The consciousness that pervades the films is a divided one— the philosophical (male) and the sensual (female) separate, incomplete, at odds, but longing for reuniting. In *The Pit and the Pendulum* we see during a montage the history of the relations between Nicholas Medina and his wife Elizabeth. The images which Corman shows in an ethereal blue-dominated flashback, come from Nicholas's own rosy memories of their "delightful conversation," "musical interludes," and other artistic/intellectual encounters that seem to preempt passion entirely. In *House of Usher,* the closest thing we see to a marital relationship is between Roderick Usher and his sister Madeleine. Madeleine's attempts to disengage herself and enter into a "normal" relationship with Philip Winthrop are thwarted by Usher to the extent that he buries her alive to avoid losing her. Human passion becomes a twisted affair (*House of Usher*) or is missing entirely (*The Pit and the Pendulum*). The desire of the male to merge with the female in sexual union becomes an obsession, but is repressed by the forces of fear, guilt, and overcivilization also at work in the male character. The male imagines the inevitable result of his desire as death, and the two are intermingled throughout the films.

All the films, from *House of Usher* to *Tomb of Ligeia*, teem with evidence of the repression of sexuality, with the gloomy mansions the characters inhabit clearly divided into two realms: the upper floors, where daily life and its "normal" activities and traditions find expression (an analogue for the superego); and the lower dungeons where the family dead reside (the attractive-repulsive realm of the id). Trips to this area become increasingly more frequent as the male character becomes more desperate to merge with the female, to self-actualize. Entrance to the crypt, nearly always, significantly, in the house rather than outside it—a "structural" symbol of death's preeminence—is usually seen in terms of a need by the tormented male—Nicholas Medina or Roderick Usher—to discover the "secret" of his own past, of the influence of evil ancestors on present conditions. This constant returning to the family crypt acts as a sort of rehearsal for sexuality, a safe version of sexual entry, since no real sexual contact occurs to threaten the powerfully isolated male.

Paradoxically, the films present death as both the alternative to the merging of the divided consciousness, and the result of it. For the tormented protagonist, merging represents a potential triumph over death, since the united consciousness will be self-actualized, hence able to defy the "natural law" of death. At the same time, this merging resonates with overwhelming fear, and the protagonist must symbolically destroy his other half in order both to avoid the merger and to transfer death to the "other" represented by his female counterpart.

The films envision death as an agonized, semi-living state offering not so much release as the denial, ever, of release from man's fears and problems. Death and life are often indistinguishable states, and the protagonists of the films tend to talk of nothing but death, and lead a kind of death-in-life existence of their own. In the "M. Valdemar" episode of *Tales of Terror*, for example, the mind continues to live in an inchoate state even while the body is decaying. In *The Pit and the Pendulum*, Elizabeth Medina appears to die twice—once when she is supposedly buried alive in the family crypt, a second time when she is locked in an Iron Maiden. In both cases she is actually alive. In *Premature Burial*, death has a far greater force and reality for Guy Carrell than life, and he exemplifies this by creating paintings that portray the world as a charnel house.

The personality of these "heroes"—a word drenched in irony when applied to men like Medina and Usher—actually dominates the films, but often from positions of weakness. Nicholas Medina, Roderick Usher, and Prince Prospero (*Masque of the Red Death*) represent different stages of personality disintegration, a theme that obsessed Corman throughout his career. Their world is a fragile one, filled with the dark rooms of their ancestral homes, a heritage they find both unbearably repulsive and sensually attractive. *House of Usher* contains the clearest embodiment of the house as an expression of the personality of its owner—complete, in this case, with an enormous crack along the side that creates frequent shakings and a constant threat of collapse. That Usher greets with derision Philip's suggestion to repair the crack shows how willingly he awaits the self-destruction it foretells.

The fear of sexuality and longing for death that exists in Corman's male characters is balanced by the desire for life in his female counterpart(s). This desire can be portrayed positively, as a maternal interest in the continuance of life (Dona Medina, Kate Carrell), or, negatively, as an impulse to destroy the male that derives in part from an unsatisfied sexuality (Elizabeth Medina, Madeleine Usher, Ligeia). The demise of the male at the hands of the female is a recurring theme that not only exemplifies Corman's obsession with male paranoia (the strong woman becomes rapaciously, murderously powerful), but also embodies the melding of death and sexuality that lies at the heart of the films.

Collaborators

The Poe films are among Corman's most successful collaborations. Certainly Corman's is the preeminent vision at work, a fact we can deduce almost mathematically by seeing the number of different, equally strong-willed writers (Richard Matheson, Charles Beaumont, R. Wright Campbell, Robert Towne, Ray Russell) whose work became, at least for the Poe films, "of a piece." David Pirie has complained that one reason *The Premature Burial* suffers is because the lead actor, Ray Milland, "comes nowhere near to attaining the *stature* that is required for this kind of role; in a way this is almost a compliment to him, for no *realistic* actor possibly could." But surely it is a tribute to Corman, and further proof of his guiding force in the films, that Milland succeeds in articulating Corman-Poe's vision, particularly during the speech that begins, "the unendurable oppression of the lungs. . . ." Corman's manipulation of the actors, sets, and camera give the films their meaning.

However, we cannot minimize the contributions of Corman's collaborators. Just as Charles Griffith and Floyd Crosby made brilliant contributions to Corman's 1950s films, so Corman found equally "willing" and talented collaborators during the following decade. Certainly what we see in the Poe films owes much of its life to Daniel Haller's densely detailed sets. At an average cost of $200,000–$300,000 (two to four times Corman's typical 1950s budgets), the Poe series have the look of much more expensive films. Haller must be credited for much of the expansive quality of what are basically claustrophobic sets. He constructed them, he has said, to allow the camera (Floyd Crosby's, in most cases), "the utmost freedom of movement."

According to Haller, "We wanted a set having many levels and ample space . . . four or five rooms were erected on the stage so they were interconnecting, and we used wide archways and stairways without balustrades. Thus the camera could move freely through the entire series of rooms for substantial takes . . . massiveness keynoted the design and construction of all sets so that the players would be dwarfed against the vast walls, and in the massive archways."[2] These comments refer specifically to *The Pit and the Pendulum*, but apply equally to other films in the series.

Floyd Crosby continued his collaboration with Corman that dated back to 1954 and *Monster from the Ocean Floor*. Corman's simple statement that "I like the idea of a moving camera" was translated by Crosby into a myriad of slow tracks and dollies, by turns elegant and unstable, particularly during those sequences detailing the descent into the lower realms of the house. Sometimes Corman and Crosby utilized a device usually considered superficial, the zip-pan, to emphasize a jarring revelation, as, for example, in the shot of Elizabeth Medina trapped in the Iron Maiden, or the extraordinary introduction of Verden Fell in *Tomb of Ligeia*.

During this period Corman and Crosby also perfected the use of laboratory opticals in Corman's films, for the montage sequences in *The Premature Burial* and *House of Usher*. *The Pit and the Pendulum* shows perhaps the finest use of this device, in the tinted montage sequences, the stretching of the image to indicate trauma during the flashback, and, particularly, during the film's major set-piece, in which the shots of the pendulum were double-printed to give the already terrifying image an overpowering density and weight.

Perhaps the most obvious—certainly visible—collaborator in the films is actor Vincent Price. Sometimes criticized for overacting, Price expresses to perfection the dissolute romantic hero of the films. Unafraid to portray extreme emotions or to embody the kind of stylized gestures required in the "unreal" world of the Poe films, Price pushed his characterizations to the limit, yet we can clearly distinguish between individual members of this gallery, and it would hardly be possible, for example, to mistake Locke in "Morella" (one episode in *Tales of Terror*) for Verden Fell in *Tomb of Ligeia,* in spite of their shared origins.

Jean-Loup Bourget has suggested approaching the films of Douglas Sirk with the idea of a "Sirk ensemble," composed not only of Sirk and his human collaborators, but also of the "storehouse of traditions" that comprised Universal Pictures,[3] the studio for whom Sirk directed most of his American pictures. This idea can be equally useful in understanding Corman. Certainly few directors were as consistent in utilizing a stock company both as actors and technicians, but Corman's ideas, even in the more high-minded Poe films, can be traced in part to the traditions of AIP and low-budget filmmaking in general. The "traditions" of AIP prior to 1960 included both genre (many horror films by Corman and other directors) and approach (limited budgets and sensational marketing). The Poe series can be said to have grown out of such earlier AIP efforts as *Attack of the Crab Monsters* or *I Was a Teenage Werewolf.* Most of AIP's artists (Haller and Crosby, for example) expanded their talents in the Poe films, and the same sense of economy that produced the earlier efforts can be seen again in *House of Usher*, though the look was so plush that Corman was taken much more seriously as a director after this film.

The Fall of the House of Usher

The House of Usher (1960) was the first Corman-Poe collaboration. Filmed at a cost of $200,000, with a primary cast of four, *House of Usher* established the conventions for all the films that followed. It marked a turning point for the director in many ways: it was the first of his films to elicit widespread (and for the most part, positive) critical reaction; it marked his shift from the subterranean depths of low-budget filmmaking to the more respectable low-to-medium (and occasionally high-) budgets and more literary, mainstream source material; and it gave full expression to Corman's feeling for mise-en-scène, a talent he perfected during the decade *House of Usher* began.

Corman's occasional color films during the 1950s[4] could not have prepared us for the sensitivity to color evident in his first Poe film, nor for his skill with the psychology of color, allowing it to express in visual and sensual form the feelings of his characters. Corman's early reputation seemed almost to depend on his use of black and white in films like *It Conquered the World, Not of This Earth,* and *Attack of the Crab Monsters.* Much of the richness of *House of Usher* and the films that followed derive from the visual aspect they present—not only in the use of color, but in the framing of shots and the use of moving camera, montage sequences, and laboratory opticals.

On the surface, *House of Usher* diverges significantly from the original source material, and purists have complained of the introduction of the "romantic" element in the person of Philip Winthrop, a fellow student of Madeleine Usher who wants to marry her. But what appears to be simply a commercial compromise takes on added dimensions as Corman sets up a lethal triangle between two men and the woman they both want to possess.

The first convention *House of Usher* establishes is the introduction of a "normal" character into an extraordinary environment, a vital character into a realm marked by images of death and decay. Here the character is Philip, but we see the same type in *The Pit and the Pendulum* (Francis Barnard), *Masque of the Red Death* (Francesca), and *Tomb of Ligeia* (Rowena), among others. The passage of this character from the normal to the abnormal world is usually rendered by means of lateral and overhead tracking shots that indicate more than a mere visit; the entry of such a character sets up a classic conflict between good and evil, a conflict that must end in the destruction of the evil, corrupt world inhabited by Usher or Medina or Prospero. The environment through which the "good," threatening character must pass is usually marked by images of vitality in desiccation, as in the fog-drenched, twisted, dead trees of *House of Usher* or *The Premature Burial*.

The second important character we see is Roderick Usher, the supersensitive aesthete who stands precariously at the center of his world. Again, the visual means by which Corman introduces this character became a standard for the films that follow. Much like the introduction of Preisig (Boris Karloff) in Ulmer's *Black Cat*, the entry of Usher into the film is rendered by a radical, unsettling technique. Whereas Ulmer cut between tracking shots to show us the perverse nature of the character, Corman uses the zip-pan to indicate the almost supernatural intensity of Usher, who (as the film validates) seems to appear and disappear without warning. The zip-pan symbolizes the loss of control as the camera moves too fast toward an object, creating an hysterical effect appropriate to a character like Usher. Usher's visage is significantly sterile; with his white hair and crimson garments he resembles a living corpse.

The Freudian tone of *House of Usher* is set early, with the striking occurrence of a mock-castration as the servant Bristol (Harry Ellerbe) asks that Philip not only remove his coat but also his boots, a request Philip finds unusual, to say the least. The abnormality of the environment, foreshadowed by Philip's passage through the rotting verdure surrounding the mansion, is signaled by Bristol's insistence on this act, and we see as the film progresses that Bristol, along with Madeleine and even the house itself, seem to carry out Usher's spoken or unspoken orders. The "de-booting" of Philip is the first of Usher's many attempts to preserve the integrity of his world.

The arrival of Madeleine from her sickbed, to interrupt a conversation between Philip and Roderick Usher, completes the triangle. If Philip represents robust good health and natural sexuality, and Roderick represents the repression of these elements, Madeleine stands somewhere between the two. Strong-willed and at least formerly healthy, Madeleine, we are told, suffers from a mysterious malady that keeps her confined to her bed. Details of this malady gradually unfold as Roderick's vague hints culminate in Philip finding Madeleine lying entranced in a coffin below the main floors of the house.

Since we know from Philip's conversation that Madeleine was healthy in Boston (and we have less reason to doubt Philip, who appears open, than Roderick, who talks in hints and innuendo), we are immediately suspicious about the reality of her "problem." As the film makes clear, Roderick, in spite of his apparent weakness, controls his insular world, and the presence of Madeleine is a *sine qua non* of that world, the female counterpart that, along with Roderick himself, must be there to comprise the total. But what is the nature of this world that Roderick feels so compelled to preserve? The house itself has several singular characteristics: it contains its own dead in the crypt below the main floors; it continues to house members of the Usher line who "made it what it is" in the form of their rotting corpses below, in the gruesome family portraits that surround Roderick in his study, and in Roderick himself. Usher's is a "world in reverse"—the inanimate is treated as, believed to be, a *living* thing (the house, the history of the family), while the actual living—Roderick and Madeleine—act out a sort of death-in-life charade that really masks Roderick's unsatisfied sexual interest in his sister.

Usher verbalizes the nature of the two worlds that exist within the film during an exquisite montage over which he explains to Philip why he cannot marry Madeleine.

It seems that before the arrival of the Ushers the land around the house was verdant. Roderick says, "Earth yielded her riches at harvest time . . . ," a phrase with unsurprising sexual connotations. Corman visualizes this with breathtaking double-exposed tracking shots through wind-stirred apple trees, dissolving into a shot of fish swimming through a brook, dissolving again as Roderick's comments take a darker turn, into a rank swamp, followed by an extreme high angle shot of the two men standing on a balcony of the house, with the split in the house's wall clearly visible behind them.

Roderick makes us aware then of the film's basic dichotomy: the world of vitality and growth, of nature following its course; and the world of murder and madness, of death and death-in-life represented by the arrival of the "cursed" Usher line. As in *The Pit and the Pendulum*, times of joy are clearly set off from the linear narrative of the film by montage sequences; thus they are only a memory rather than the present reality. And, like Nicholas Medina and others in the Corman-Poe constellation, Roderick wholeheartedly embraces the splendidly appointed but hopeless existence of which life, for him, consists.

As Roderick rejects the more positive world (figuratively and literally, by cloistering himself from the world at large and carrying on a too-close relationship with his sister), he creates his own alternate version. He is an artist, a creator; he paints gruesome (and significantly, modern, ahistorical) portraits, emphasizing simultaneously a quality of despair and one of raging, blood-spattered sexuality. He plays stylized "songs" which Philip pretends to appreciate. Most important, he exerts a strong, if constantly threatened, control over Madeleine. His descriptions of her personality, however, do not seem so much inherent qualities in Madeleine as, again, part of Roderick's own, ultimately successful, re-creation of her personality to flesh out the other half of his world.

For example, he claims that the same disease which afflicts him—a nervous condition that renders all sensation, but particularly hearing, unbearable—also plagues his sister. The film contradicts this as Philip says that in Boston, far from being sick, she was "exuberant" and "full of the joy of living." Her "sickness" seems to have begun when she returned home—for unexplained reasons that hardly need explaining. The image she actually presents is one of vitality and power, and a vivid sexuality in her scenes with Philip. However, under her brother's influence, she grows more pliable, more willing to accept his descriptions of her. He veils his fear of her being taken away from him with the explanation that all the Usher blood is tainted and that the most broad, humane thing would be to let the line die out—hence his attempts to block her exit with Philip.

True to the spirit of Poe, the film portrays the relationship of the pair as quasi-incestuous, with Usher contradicting the vibrant image we see of Madeleine in order to couple herself with him. Like lovers, they share "secret knowledge" at the dinner table, when Madeleine gives signs to her brother not to reveal their family history or evidence of her "disease," their "secrets." Philip represents two things in relation to this "couple": an avenue of escape for Madeleine from her brother and his neurosis; and the destruction of the fragile, insular world of Usher in the face of Philip's utter normalcy and adjustment to life. Confronted with Usher's bizarre behavior and the sordid family history, Philip charitably insists they were merely evidencing "pecu-

larities of temperament." Ridiculed by Roderick for wanting to repair
the enormous crack up the side of the house, Philip explains his rea-
soning with simple eloquence: "for Madeleine's safety."

Roderick's need to possess his sister, to retain her as the ultimate
icon in his world—the beautiful but untouchable female, vibrant yet
"cataleptic," sexual yet unapproachable—increases as Philip's tenacity
continues, and the struggle between the two men for possession of
Madeleine accelerates. When it becomes clear that she plans to dis-
obey her brother and leave with Philip, Roderick finds a unique way
out of his problem: he can keep her in the house at once "alive" and
"dead." When Philip hears her scream after an argument between Madeleine and Roderick, he enters her room to find Roderick standing
away from the bed, saying "she's dead." Philip learns later, from Bristol, that she suffered from catalepsy. During the funeral service, Corman shows us what Roderick knows: that Madeleine is really alive, but
in a cataleptic trance. When Roderick sees her fingers move within her
coffin, an action Corman shows in the foreground, Roderick hastens to
close the coffin and transport it to the family crypt below. This and the
scene that follows comprise the obligatory scene, recurring in most of
the series, showing the mock-destruction of the female by the male
that gives the ostensible motive for the female's ultimate revenge. In
The Pit and the Pendulum this scene exists as a flashback in which
Sebastian Medina chains his wife inside a wall, alive. In *House of Usher* Corman visualizes the same kind of scene with an optical track into
Madeleine's name on her coffin, with the surrounding area of the frame
darkened, followed by Madeleine's long scream as she realizes she has
been buried alive.

At this point the film, which has built slowly, concentrating on the
atmosphere of the house and character details, accelerates as Roderick
has finally acted to preserve the sanctity of his world by killing his
sister. The advantages of this act to Roderick are several: it theoreti-
cally removes the threat of Philip, since with Madeleine gone he has
no clear reason to be there; it preserves his world by maintaining the
presence of Madeleine, even though nominally dead, in the house; it
removes the tension of sexuality from Roderick; and it confirms Roderick's godlike power, his superiority, in imposing death and life, indeed, in blurring these states since Madeleine can be construed as
both. However, nothing works quite as planned. Philip stubbornly refuses to leave, and Madeleine refuses to stay dead. The feared-desired
"coming together" of Madeleine and Roderick occurs, in the film's climactic set-piece of Madeleine's bloody "resurrection."

Roderick has warned Philip that most of his family became insane
and "in their madness it took the power of many to subdue them." This
is what happens to Madeleine. Driven crazy by having been locked in

The final bloody encounter between Roderick and Madeleine Usher (Vincent Price and Myrna Fahey).

the coffin (a symbol not only of death but of blocked sexuality), Madeleine rends open her tomb and, dripping blood throughout the house, makes her way toward Roderick. A temporary encounter with Philip leaves him dazed on the floor. Roderick, aware of exactly what is happening, takes out a gun, but drops it as Madeleine enters the room. A fallen lamp ignites a curtain, and the fire spreads throughout the house. In the midst of flaming walls and collapsing rafters we see Madeleine and Roderick in a tight embrace, but with Madeleine's hands locked securely around his throat. Philip escapes with the aid of Bristol, but the brother and sister die in each other's arms in the house.

Most of the films that followed in the series contain this kind of climax, in which the sexual tensions in the important male character find ultimate release. The films express the Freudian idea (the child's fear) that sexuality ends in death. And death means not only the death of the individual, but the death of the world itself, since in Corman's work the world is created by the individual consciousness.

The Pit and the Pendulum

Corman chose as his second Poe project *The Pit and the Pendulum* (1961). Like its predecessor, the original story is a powerful mood study, with little in the way of "action" or recognizable "characters," concerning the psychological disintegration of an Inquisition victim. The transition from story to screen required a whole new plot, and characters that could express Poe's concepts without being entirely submissive to them. The result is one of Corman's most powerful films, a near-perfect marriage of formal devices and themes.

The Pit and the Pendulum recalls *House of Usher* from the onset, with the arrival of a normal character into an abnormal, insular environment. The character is Francis Barnard (John Kerr), arriving at the mansion of Nicholas Medina (Vincent Price) to investigate the mysterious death of his sister, Nicholas's wife Elizabeth (Barbara Steele). Unlike *House of Usher*, Corman visualizes this as a passage from the real world (this sequence begins with a true exterior shot by the ocean, not a studio shot as in the previous film) into a world of apparent corruption and death. Again, Corman signals the mythic nature of this arrival by shooting it with an overhead crane. As in *House of Usher*, there is an initial resistance on the part of a servant to allow the visitor access to the mansion or its inhabitants. As always, these servants are mere ciphers acting out the wishes of their masters, not so much in waiting on them as in protecting them from the intrusions of the outside world. Because the visitors to these environments are not merely visitors, but agents of destruction, they cannot be kept back by servants. These are archetypal dramas that pit good against evil, with the "good" embodied by only one person subjecting himself or herself to the rigors of the corrupt world, designated formally by montage sequences or overdubs that contrast a past, now dead world of good, with the present decadent conditions.

Again, at the center of this world stands a faltering figure, the guilt-ridden sexually tormented aesthete, Nicholas Medina, who longs for the pleasures of sexual union yet is paralyzed by the prospect. As in *House of Usher*, some blame is laid at the door of the past, with "depraved blood" blamed for the aesthete's supposed crime of having buried his wife alive. The first thing we learn about Elizabeth, after hearing she is dead, is that she has "no grave," that she is "interred below," by family custom, that is, she is in the house, residing in its consciousness, believed dead. Nicholas Medina's abrupt entry confirms the obsession with death that runs throughout this film when he replies to Francis Barnard that the "device" whose noisy machinery has been heard "must be kept in constant repair," an alarming fact considering that the Inquisition, which utilized the machine, ended years ago.

Francis Barnard's sneering disbelief creates a more hostile atmosphere in *The Pit and the Pendulum* than in the earlier film. Where Philip and Roderick seemed almost evenly matched, Francis seems more powerful than the deteriorating Nicholas. As the story unfolds we learn that Nicholas and Elizabeth were once happy, but that "something" came between them. This turns out to be Elizabeth's obsession with the castle, in whose depths mass tortures were carried out by Nicholas's infamous father, Sebastian. Francis Barnard's constant harping on "what really happened," his insistence that Nicholas has "an air of definite guilt," trigger further revelations. We learn that Nicholas as a child saw his mother tortured to death, a "fact" later amended by the family physician, Dr. Leon, to her being tortured, then buried alive. These are the ostensible influences on Nicholas's life, on his inability, as his sister puts it, "to live as other men."

Corman contrasts these past events with the present by enclosing them in lurid montage sequences shot with color filters and various laboratory opticals. The first montage we see is a key one, wherein the "happy" relations between Nicholas and Elizabeth are shown. Little passionate behavior seems to have occurred, and the couple's time was mostly spent with Nicholas waiting on Elizabeth, bringing her breakfast in bed each morning, attempting "in vain" to capture her beauty on canvas, and otherwise canonizing her. They enjoyed "intimate conversations, sometimes alone and sometimes with the doctor." At this point the camera pans to the right to show the doctor, with Elizabeth turning away from Nicholas toward the doctor. Life was, as Nicholas says in his overdub that accompanies the montage, "simple, quiet, richly pleasurable." In his introduction to the montage, he calls their life "good, rich with the shared pleasures of our love," but we see little evidence of passion or eroticism, a key factor that offers some clue of why Elizabeth and Dr. Leon concoct the elaborate scheme not only of running away together, but of driving Nicholas insane as well. Nicholas's own views of his relations with Elizabeth seem to reflect more a desire for family relations than a marital one, providing the close communion of a family without the burden of sexuality associated with mature, marital relations. As the montage continues we see Elizabeth's supposed descent into madness, in which "the castle and its awful history had obsessed her." This is an elaborate montage, the first of three, in which the blue monochrome tint is disrupted only at the end when Elizabeth falls "dead" out of an Iron Maiden with the name "Sebastian" on her lips. At this point the color changes suddenly to purple. In addition to the striking use of color, the montage contains tracking shots and shock cuts, as well as extremely stylized "acting," particularly by Barbara Steele as Elizabeth. In the unreal world of the Poes, and the doubly unreal world of this montage within the film, Elizabeth's unnatural movements, falling backward into Nicholas's arms or lurching forward onto a torture object with which she has become fascinated, create the image of a puppet moving inscrutably at the behest of an unseen force, surely a perfect visual analogue for the mysterious manipulations of mankind by an unseen, unknown God.

The Pit and the Pendulum supports the idea of an indifferent, or inscrutable creator more fully than does *House of Usher*. Both films contain religious imagery, but *The Pit and the Pendulum*, like *Masque of the Red Death* two years later, seems to be partly about the estrangement of mankind from God. Two aspects of the film support this. The first is a poetic montage comprised of tracks and dissolves, in which the camera surveys various aspects of the castle, concentrating mostly on torture objects like the Iron Maiden and the rack, and on religious icons placed throughout. This coupling of Sebastian Medina's implements of destruction with seemingly innocent, hopeful images of Christ on the Cross and an elaborate altarpiece makes its point. There is no "linear" (plot) excuse for this scene, though Corman links it with the plot per se by underscoring it with music being played by the "dead" Elizabeth. The montage melds into a tracking shot that rests on Francis Barnard, startled by the harpsichord music he has heard.

The other strong religious reference occurs during the climactic set-piece, the near-destruction of Francis Barnard at the hands of the "possessed" Nicholas. Nicholas, believing he is his father Sebastian, delivers the important speech that defines his world and the viewpoint of the film. This is a speech we find in all the Poe films, though it is most clearly set off in *House of Usher, The Premature Burial*, and the present film. This speech will be discussed below in the context of the film's climax.

The Pit and the Pendulum is probably Corman's most montage-heavy film. Certainly few others contain so many complex, formal montage sequences. According to Herb Lightman, "The finished [montage] sequences were printed on blue-tinted stock which were then toned red during development, producing the effect of a two-tone image—the highlights went blue, while the shadows (represented by areas where more emulsion was present) held the dye and were rendered as red, producing a realistic bloody quality. To further enhance the atmosphere of horror, the image was then run through an optical printer where the edges were vignetted and a twisted linear distortion was introduced."

The second key montage occurs while Catherine (Luana Anders), Nicholas's sister, is talking to Francis, trying to convince him to believe

Nicholas's story that Elizabeth died of "fright" and that he had nothing to do with her death. As a revelation of Nicholas's character, the earlier montage goes further in suggesting that Elizabeth's revenge derives from Nicholas's inability to satisfy her sexually (indeed, with separate bedrooms there is no real evidence that they have even slept together). As a formal device that defines the influence of the past on Nicholas, and shows from the child's viewpoint the destruction of the mother at the hands of the father, the second montage is as powerful as anything in Corman's work.

As in the first montage, Corman begins this montage during a speech by one of the key characters, whose remembrances comprise the montage. However, whereas in the earlier one he blackened the screen around the character's eyes, then expanded it into a full-screen montage, he only expands the second montage partially, retaining the sense of a field of vision, of eyes looking into the past. Again he uses a monochrome tint of blue, and the first thing we see on the left side of the frame is a small area in which a ball is bouncing along a stone stairway. Catherine's overdub tells us that it is a toy of Nicholas's that he accidentally drops into his father's torture chamber. Expressly forbidden to enter, "the curiosity of youth" overcame his fear and he entered. As the ball rolls along, Corman expands the screen by showing young Nicholas pursuing the ball, within a blue field of a shape approximating the field of human vision. Eventually the screen expands and Nicholas wanders about touching the various torture instruments. This is significant because it is also the way Nicholas would later portray for Francis Barnard Elizabeth's descent into madness (an indication of Nicholas's selfish, self-created world in which he "plays all parts"). Nicholas's investigation is disturbed by the entry of his father with his mother Isabella and his uncle Bartolome. It seems Sebastian is giving the pair a "ghastly tour" of the torture chamber, and Nicholas hides while this tour is occurring. Nicholas becomes nervous, we are told, with a "mounting sense of premonition" that something terrible will occur, and as he watches, Sebastian reaches for a red-hot poker with which he slashes Bartolome. Corman signals the violence of this moment with an abrupt cut to Isabella screaming. The color shifts with equal abruptness from blue to a crimson red, and Corman further compounds the traumatic feeling by stretching the image. Her screams are somewhat disembodied, not entirely matching the movements of her mouth, and counterpointed further by Catherine's overdub in the background, almost forgotten in the midst of what is happening visually. Sebastian has murdered Bartolome and is walling up his wife alive in repayment for their adulterous affair. Corman alternates red and blue filters throughout the last shots of these violent events, and expands the horror by stretching the images of the screaming woman,

the hooded, Satanic-appearing Sebastian, and the innocent, terrified
Nicholas. As the montage ends and we return to the present, Catherine says, "And there before my brother's eyes, our mother was tortured to death."

Nicholas's presence at this event seems to have altered his ability
"to live as other men," according to his sister. He is "obsessed with
guilt" at what occurred, the powerless feeling of the child who, in psychoanalytic terms, fails to "save" his mother from the sexual, seemingly
murderous assault of the father. Indeed, our first view of Nicholas confirms his masochism, when he tells the hostile Francis Barnard that
"you have every right to be suspicious." Nicholas is weak, his personality on the verge of disintegration, ready to be taken over by whatever
stronger force—the "ghost" of Sebastian, of his "tainted blood," or
Elizabeth—happens to come along. Corman structures this montage
in clearly Freudian terms, with the alternation of blue into red signaling the beginning of the feared destruction of the mother by the rapacious father, while the son looks helplessly on. This is a psychic zone
we are in, an area of memory from nearly preconscious days that has a
crippling effect on the events of the present. Nicholas's apparent inability to satisfy Elizabeth stems from the violent separation of himself
from his mother, the destruction of his mother at the hands of his father, and his symbolic castration by the same man.

Dr. Leon informs Francis Barnard and Catherine of a "secret" that
only Nicholas and himself were previously aware of: his mother was
tortured, "but not to death." She was first tortured, then buried alive,
a fact that has compounded Nicholas's miserable condition. Corman
reprises the montage by showing the image of Nicholas's mother,
bloody and enchained but still alive, being walled up in the torture
chamber of the house. As in most of the Poe films, past events appear
more vivid and real to the protagonist than the dreary present. Not
only does the past influence the present, it actually preempts it as
Nicholas Medina, in a paroxysm of masochism, re-creates in detail the
key traumatic events of his past. Already a weak, hysterical personality,
the news that he may have buried his wife alive, as Sebastian did his
mother, threatens to push him over the edge. The film plays with our
perception of Nicholas—is he crazy?—by showing various manifesta-
tions of Elizabeth's continued presence: the playing of the harpsichord,
one of her rings discovered on the instrument, a servant overhearing
"the mistress" saying "Leave this room!" Finally, Nicholas, Francis,
Catherine, and Dr. Leon decide to disinter Elizabeth, to see if perhaps
she really is alive.

House of Usher established the convention of the descent "down"
into the bowels of the house, where the family dead are buried "according to custom." This event, far from being a mere plot device to

discover whether or not a character was dead when buried, becomes a rite of passage for the tormented protagonist, whose mental stability seems to depend on the verification of his own control or lack thereof. All the films view the human personality as a thing trapped within levels. The first level is the body, dying as soon as it is born, or simultaneously alive and dead (M. Valdemar, Elizabeth Medina). The second is another kind of carapace, the coffin or crypt in which the body resides. The mental stability of the protagonist seems to depend on this encounter with the dead, but the encounter is in fact a violent attack on the "body" represented by the coffin, both a repudiation of death and a substitution for the penetration of sexuality. Only after this event occurs can the conflicts within the character be resolved. Hence we have Nicholas attacking the wall behind which his wife is interred, breaking it down stone by stone, opening the casket to discover a gruesome, desiccated body with hands upraised in a clawing motion. This apparent revelation that Elizabeth was buried alive represents the point at which Nicholas's personality begins to disappear entirely, allowing for the formation of a new personality, based on his remembrances of Sebastian's activities.

For the first time we glimpse Elizabeth Medina, alive, as she lures Nicholas into the "pit," a place with clear Freudian resonance. Nicholas's castration anxiety is played upon by Elizabeth, who seems to understand her husband's masochism and to wish to act on it. Even after Nicholas has collapsed into catatonia, and Elizabeth's lover Dr. Leon is urging her to leave the castle with him, she cannot resist torturing him. Thus she is willing to endanger herself and the game she and Dr. Leon have played in cuckolding Nicholas, in order to further degrade her husband. Here we see to perfection the Corman-Poe rapacious female, a more extraordinary example in this film than in *House of Usher,* where there was a logical as well as a psychological basis for Madeleine's murder of her brother. Elizabeth is like Ligeia in *Tomb of Ligeia,* an archetypal image of the destructive rather than nurturing feminine principle. The death of Nicholas's mother left the child (which Nicholas has never ceased to be as evidenced by his childlike, dependent, even servile behavior toward Elizabeth in the first montage) without defenses against the rampaging father (which Nicholas becomes) or the sensuous female represented by Elizabeth, who tortures Nicholas, amused at his own weakness, his inability to act.

The film moves into its climax when Elizabeth reminds Nicholas of the "amusing" parallels between the events of the past and those of the present: "Is it not ironic . . . your wife an adulteress, your mother an adulteress, your uncle an adulterer, your closest friend an adulterer? Do you not find that amusing?" Elizabeth, whom we have seen only as a shadow-figure, manifested in mysterious harpsichord music, and the whispered name, "Nicholas," as she lured him into the pit, emerges as a very living, blood-spattered woman who spends no little time tormenting her husband. There is again no "logical" reason why she should torment him. After all, she and the doctor have merely planned to rob Nicholas and run away together. But when Dr. Leon, more pragmatic, tells her that "There is no time for this," she contradicts him with a strange line, "I've waited an eternity for this moment. There has to be time!" Thus we see Elizabeth is not merely interested in cuckolding Nicholas, or robbing him; she wants to punish him, but why?

First we must remember that the world of *The Pit and the Pendulum* is above all the world of Nicholas Medina. His consciousness pervades the house. He keeps the torture objects below "in constant repair," as he says. He chose each object in Elizabeth's room, furnishing her world for her. Hence the activities of those around him must be analyzed in light of Nicholas's fears and desires. The major event in his life seems to be his helplessly witnessing the destruction of his mother. Elizabeth's insistence on torturing him can be read on one level as the revenge of the mother against the child who stood by passively watching her being tortured and killed. The parallels between Elizabeth and Isabella verify this. Both were adulteresses, both apparently prematurely interred. The image of the "corpse" of Elizabeth, frozen in a posture of agony, is matched by Nicholas's remembrance of his mother, in bloody rags, chained screaming to the wall. Elizabeth, too, is associated with blood. The first glimpse Nicholas has of the real Elizabeth is her bloody hand reaching out of the coffin. Above all, this is Nicholas's world, and his wife embodies Nicholas's impulse toward self-destruction, his guilt at having allowed his father to murder his mother. When Elizabeth says to Nicholas, "I have you exactly where I want you . . . helpless," she is putting Nicholas in his mother's place, tortured by one from whom love, rather than violence, was expected.

Elizabeth's torture does not have the desired effect, as her mentioning of the—for Nicholas—resonant names from the past—"your mother, your father"—triggers a collapse of Nicholas's personality into his father's. Nicholas's obsession with the castle is far more real than Elizabeth's (and we recall that he with typical egoism initially blamed "the castle and its awful history" on her demise, transferring his feelings to her), and has paved the way for our acceptance of this turnaround. Nicholas stands, kills Dr. Leon by banging his head against a wall, then locks his faithless wife in a nearby Iron Maiden. Significantly, the only sign of overt sexuality we see in Nicholas occurs at this point, where his personality has dissolved. Being suddenly reborn as Sebastian allows Nicholas to passionately embrace and kiss his bloody wife, while describing the fate he has in store for her: "You'll beg me to kill you to relieve you of the agony of hell into which your husband is about to plunge you."

Corman has defined the world of the film—Nicholas's world—in visual terms throughout, and iconographic images such as tombs, spider webs, rats, rotting vegetation already familiar from *House of Usher* are repeated in *The Pit and the Pendulum*. But these films also contain a key speech that states in extreme terms what comprises the world the protagonist inhabits, a world of utter bleakness, of man deserted, even tortured by God, unable to emerge from a state of childhood trauma into self-actualization. When Nicholas "becomes" Sebastian, escaping the confused impulses of his previous character, he recites a speech that brings together the sexual and philosophical elements of the film. The scene is the torture chamber; Nicholas has mistaken Francis Barnard for his adulterous brother in one of the film's several identity transfers, and has chained him beneath a vast, razor-sharp pendulum that will slowly cut him in half while he is alive. Barnard is tied to an "island" that shoots up out of the pit, in the lowest realm of the house. The walls of this area, "the pit," display vaguely human hooded images that could be Nicholas's tainted ancestors, or monk-like representatives of a God by turns indifferent and destructive. Nicholas-Sebastian has confused Francis for his dead uncle Bartolome, and is ready to reenact the early torture of that long-dead character. Here is his speech: "Now we are ready to begin. . . . Do you know where you are, Bartolome? I will tell you where you are. You are about to enter hell, Bartolome. Hell! The netherworld . . . the infernal regions . . . the abode of the damned, the place of torment. . . . Pandemonium. . . . Gehenna. . . . Naraka. . . . the pit! And the pendulum . . . the razor edge of death. Thus the condition of man, bound on an island from which he can never hope to escape, surrounded by the waiting pit of hell. . . ." This extraordinary speech precedes Nicholas's use of his "ultimate device of torture," the pendulum. It is hardly accidental that the final, most potent synonym he uses for life/hell is "the pit," considering the heavy element of castration anxiety in the film. For Nicholas "the pit," the fear of sexuality, does represent the ultimate horror. Like Roderick Usher, sexual desire becomes an impossibility, at least until he can confront it in the guise of Sebastian Medina. The pendulum itself is a monstrous construct we have only encountered aurally before the climax. It creates a wrenching sound that disturbs Francis Barnard almost immediately upon entering the Medina house. In the final sequence he finds himself chained beneath it, awaiting mutilation and death. The pendulum itself acts as a double symbol in the scheme of the film. Most obviously it counterpoints the pit as a phallic symbol, but specifically linked to Sebastian Medina who, through the person of Nicholas, controls it; thus, the violent, castrating

*Daniel Haller's most elaborate set for the Poe series—the psychic zone of the Poe/
Corman hero* (The Pit and the Pendulum).

father. On another level it represents time's rapaciousness, since the
object exists normally in a clock, marking the passage of time. Time
for Corman's Poe characters merely means moving closer and closer to
death.

According to Daniel Haller, the pendulum set "occupied a whole
sound stage and stretched from the floor to the rafters." It was further
augmented on the screen by matte additions, to give the look of an
extremely massive environment. Haller continues, "The camera was
mounted on a parallel at the opposite end of the stage and a 40mm
Panavision wide-angle lens used," enabling "Crosby to frame the scene
in his camera with extra space allowed at the bottom and at either side.
These areas were then filled in later by printing-in process extensions
of the set, effectively doubling its size."[5]

Corman reserved some of his most telling visual strategies for the
final sequence. Once Nicholas starts the pendulum, nearly all of the
shots are timed to the swinging of this monstrous object, an unusual
style for a director more devoted to moving camera than montage. The
effect of all the cutting between the pendulum, the chained Francis

Barnard, the ghastly walls of the pit, and the crazed Nicholas, creates an unrelieved atmosphere of tension and gloom. Corman carries this further with his use of wide-angle distortions, kiltered angles, and, most particularly, laboratory opticals in which the image of the pendulum, viewed mostly from Francis's point of view, was double printed to add density to an already overpowering image.

Earlier in the film Corman introduced sporadically an image from outside the castle, a conventional shot of waves breaking against the shore below. In an archetypal drama detailing the struggle of good and evil this image, reminding us of the world outside that of Nicholas and his obsessions, represents the continuity of the other, more healthy world. The triumph of that world occurs when Catherine and one of the servants manage to break into the pit, to free Francis Barnard just at the point of his mutilation by the pendulum, and to push the insane Nicholas into the pit still alive (his eyes, bloodstained, are open). In a neat parallel plot device, the script has only the principals of the drama—Nicholas, Elizabeth, Dr. Leon—knowing what really happened, and Dr. Leon is dead, Nicholas certainly near death in the pit, but Elizabeth definitely alive—gagged—in the Iron Maiden. When Catherine shuts the door to the pit and says "No one will ever enter this room again," Corman violently zip-pans to the image of Elizabeth, her eyes visible and wide open, but unable to scream. In the film's final irony, no attempt is made to free her because no one except Nicholas and Dr. Leon knew she was alive.

The Premature Burial

The Premature Burial (1961), the third film in the series, received more than a little negative criticism, even from devotees of Corman. David Pirie, writing in *Roger Corman: The Millennic Vision*, refers to the film as "a self-evident disaster,"[6] blaming the replacement of Vincent Price with Ray Milland for part of the film's failure. However, the use of a "realistic" actor like Milland actually gives the film much of its power, and in some ways pushes the film farther than its two predecessors in creating an atmosphere of unrelieved grimness. Unlike Price, who usually seems less in conflict with than a part of the decadent, stifling world he inhabits, Milland appears more as a normal person caught in circumstances far beyond his control—the "real" person trapped in an artificial environment. Whereas Roderick Usher and Nicholas Medina appear to have created the world they inhabit and derive obvious satisfactions from it, Guy Carrell in *The Premature Burial* appears clearly as the victim of this world. As usual, Corman completely encloses the world of the film, and the exteriors show a land as dead as the well-appointed crypt or the suffocating red-brown bedroom Guy inhabits. Guy stumbles through this world, paralyzed with a fear of being "buried alive."

The plot centers on the return of a rejected suitor, Emily Gault (Hazel Court), to Guy's life. We learn that Guy has tried to send her away because he is "sick," afflicted with catalepsy, a disease that re-creates the symptoms of death in a living person, threatening him with premature burial. Guy is obsessed with the idea that his father was buried alive, though his protective sister Kate, the "voice of reason" throughout the film, disputes this. The film plays a game with the audience in not clarifying who is behind the campaign to drive Guy to insanity or death by playing on his fears. It implies that Guy himself may be responsible, since he is simultaneously attracted and repelled by death; or it may be Kate, who remains a somewhat mysterious figure throughout, appearing at key points as if from nowhere, administering laudanum to Guy, who, like Roderick Usher, must take drugs to sleep; or it may be Emily, though the film is careful to show the utter solicitousness of her character. Indeed, the final revelation that it is Emily who has triggered Guy's premature burial comes as no small surprise.

The signs of Emily's true nature are implied visually throughout, however, as we look back through the film. As with Madeleine Usher and Elizabeth Medina, we are dealing with a highly sexual character, a woman who appears to have maternal instincts in both a positive and negative sense: positive in sheltering Guy from the horrors of his own world, negative in the connotation of smothering. Corman verifies the latter in the way he positions the characters in the frame. Guy is frequently seen retreating after a "spell" to his oppressively funereal room, stretching out in a passive way on the bed. When Emily follows him there for the first time, she hovers over him. He remains still, and her figure dominates, eventually covering his image in the frame with her own. Subtle reactions to a discussion with Dr. Miles Archer, a family friend, about the precarious nature of Guy's mental balance, also provide a clue to Emily's nature. She seems to drink in, without revealing too much, his statement that she must be careful not to be "suggestive" with Guy, to avoid references to death, his father, and other spurs to trauma. Corman also uses color to indicate Emily's real attitude. When we first see her, she is contrasted with Kate. Both women wear black dresses, but Emily also wears a black hat with excessive red frills that almost seem alive. Yet another clue comes when Emily and Miles rescue a kitten "prematurely buried" in one of the walls of the mansion. Guy is the first to hear its pitiful cry, and he watches in horror as the living creature is rescued from behind the wall. Emily puts the cat around her neck, "wearing" it as she might a—dead—fox fur.

But why should Emily want to destroy him? As with her predecessor, Elizabeth Medina, the reasons seem complex, with a surface motivation easily giving way to a more complex one. To discover this, we need to look at the world that Guy Carrell inhabits.

As so often in the Poe films, the "world" of the action is delineated in many ways, visual, verbal, musical. The first scene in the film shows Guy Carrell and Emily's father (also a doctor) watching two "filthy graverobbers," as Guy describes them, opening a grave. Guy watches with morbid fascination as the image of the man inside the coffin comes to light, an image Corman freezes on—a tautly stretched man now dead but obviously buried alive. The title flashes on top of this image, indicating from the onset the bleak nature of the film.

Corman also inserts in the early passages the obligatory speech by the tormented protagonist that verbally defines this world: "Can you possibly imagine it? The unendurable oppression of the lungs . . . the stifling fumes of the earth . . . the rigid embrace of the coffin . . . the blackness of absolute night . . . and the silence like an overwhelming sea. And then, invisible, but all too real to the senses, the presence of the conqueror worm." This speech comes almost verbatim from Poe, one of the few things in the virtually plotless original story that screenwriters Charles Beaumont and Ray Russell could use.

As so often in the Poe series, Corman makes the main character an artist, an overly sensitive being who, as he says himself, "knows the truth." In *The Premature Burial*, Guy spends some of his time painting, but initially we only see the briefest snippets of his work, which recalls Francis Bacon in its depiction of the body as a shell of flesh and blood. When Emily insists on seeing his latest work, she also helps to satisfy the audience's desire to see what kind of universe Guy portrays. He hesitates, then uncovers the painting, revealing a cartoon-Boschian world of demons, spirits, and cannibals, with a huge Satanic image dominating. The camera lingers on this image, recalling the paintings in *House of Usher* which offered similar yet far less emphatic images of human degradation and entrapment.

Corman's use of the musical leitmotiv, "Molly Malone," deserves some examination. The multiple uses of this apparently harmless tune would seem to indicate a purpose beyond adding a mere gloomy touch, and the lyrics, particularly the refrain, bear this out. The song first appears in the opening scene, as a background whistle from one of the graverobbers. Emily insistently plays it at the wedding party, triggering one of Guy's attacks. The song recurs later when Guy alone seems to hear it, whereupon he follows the sound through the gloomy moors surrounding his mansion, an episode that ends in yet another attack. The refrain to the song, which portrays a street vendor selling her

The Premature Burial: *(top) Guy Carrell (Ray Milland), upright, creative; (bottom) prone, passive, waiting.*

wares, is "alive-o, alive-o." As we come to see that life, rather than death, constitutes the biggest threat to Guy, the song takes on great significance.

The strongest images of Guy's world, however, come directly from his environment, both indoors and out. Obsessed with death, he furnishes his house in oppressive browns and reds, that seem to have the double connotation of a Freudian womb-fantasy and the very earth that he feels waits to envelop him. His room is an extremely enclosed retreat, and he assumes a position of rigid passivity on his bed. The "outdoors" is hardly more comforting. As in *House of Usher*, Guy's mansion is surrounded by twisted, dead trees constantly drenched in a swirling fog. The "romantic" walks that Guy and Emily take throughout this environment take on an ironic note due to its utter deadness. Exteriors and interiors are equally claustrophobic, since even the exteriors are invented, artificial, and enclosed.

Typically, this insular, decadent world teeters on the brink of destruction. The agent of destruction usually arrives in the opening minutes of the film—sometimes a positive character (*House of Usher*, *Tomb of Ligeia*), sometimes seemingly positive, as in *The Premature Burial*. We learn late in the film that Emily was a woman who always "wanted to be a great lady," and this offers us some clue as the surface reason for her entry into Guy's life and her attempts to destroy it. But Corman gives us another reason for her mysterious behavior. As in *House of Usher* or *The Pit and the Pendulum*, the world of *The Premature Burial* reflects the obsessions of the main character. Unlike the previous films, however, Guy Carrell is not in control of this world, even though he has in some sense created it. He alternates between bleak-to-hopeless renderings of his world in his paintings, his "morbid" creation of an escapable crypt, his fear-motivated trips to the moors, his fear of leaving the environment by going on a vacation. But the world he inhabits is beyond his control; he is its victim. The pain of his suffering is stated emphatically during one of his attacks, when Corman shows him racing up a staircase, pausing and lowering his head, with the image of the first prematurely buried man superimposed on him, then dissolving. Guy's weakness implies impotence, a suggestion furthered by Corman's placement of Guy in positions of subordination to Emily in the frame. Thus we can see Emily's desire to kill Guy not only to assume his wealth but as punishment for his weakness, his inability to satisfy her. This is further validated by the psychic zone in which the drama is played out—the rooms consciously colored and furnished to suggest an intrauterine space, with Emily acting as a rapacious mother figure, punishing the "son" (Guy) for his preemption of his father. (And Guy does become his father in the most significant way, since he is also *buried alive*.)

Guy vacillates throughout the film between his desire to "rest in peace" (the last words of the film) and his desire to act, to escape his own paralyzing fears. For Guy, the problem of death is that it may not be real, that it offers a false hope of release. As a therapeutic act, he creates an elaborate crypt that has a variety of ingenious escape routes, from a coffin containing escape devices to dynamite to a ladder that falls from the ceiling. He sardonically offers Emily and Miles a tour of this environment, which both find repugnant, lovingly displaying each of its novel features. The final touch, the "piece de resistance, or should I say the coup de grace?" he offers as "the cure for all suffering . . . the key to heaven, or to hell, or to nothingness . . . poison." This seemingly morbid creation actually represents a positive attempt by Guy to deal with his fears, but Emily, threatened by it, enlists Miles's help in convincing him to destroy it. Shortly thereafter he again suffers an attack and is buried alive.

Corman uses a variety of formal devices here to elucidate his theme. Jerry Kutner has suggested that many of Corman's films contain a unifying formal device that reflects his ideas.[7] He cites, for example, the use of elaborate tracking shots in *The Haunted Palace* to emphasize that film's obsession with time. In *The Premature Burial*, the preeminent device is the shock cut. The usual transition here is from a relatively peaceful shot, for example, an embrace or a static alignment of characters, to a traumatic movement of some kind. For example, when Miles and Emily are discussing the possibility that Guy's father was actually buried alive, the camera pans over to Kate, who disputes this. She says, "My father rests in peace," and Corman cuts immediately to a wrenching shot of Guy in bed, lunging feverishly up toward the camera. Another combination of mobile and static images in a shock cut is the scene mentioned earlier when Guy runs up a staircase during an attack, and when he pauses, moving his head slowly down in a posture of despair, Corman cuts to the freeze-frame of the prematurely buried man, then dissolves back to Guy.

At the same time, Corman does not neglect formal montage or moving camera. In one of the greatest set-pieces in the entire series, he shows Guy collapsing on the moors, then passing into a "dream." The dream, shot in lush blue and green filters, returns us to Guy's well-furnished crypt, but in the dream the interior of the crypt and all its furnishings have rotted. Spiders and rats crawl about, and Guy himself is frozen in the coffin. During his earlier demonstration of the crypt for Emily and Miles he told them how only "a slight movement of my finger" could cause the coffin to spring open. In the dream-montage it will not open, until his violent movements cause it to fall from its stand and break. Desperate, he tests each of his escape methods, but finds them all rotted or useless. Even his "piece de resistance," the goblet of poison, contains only white worms. This scene provides a perfect metaphor for death as its own prison, offering not release or oblivion but a living state of entrapment and utter, unwilling solitude. Corman compounds this image by initially showing Guy not only trapped in the coffin but mute, his inability to speak punctuated ironically by horn sounds that accompany his vain attempts to scream.

The film also contains much mobile camerawork, particularly effective in the scenes where Guy "hears something" in the moors and pursues it. The camera alternates between overhead and horizontal tracks, drawing the character ever closer to his own demise. In the scenes of his actual burial, Corman combines moving camera with point-of-view shots, as Guy lies with what seem to be open eyes, looking through the glass window of his coffin, watching the image of his family and friends receding as he is lowered into the ground. At this point another shock movement (without a cut) occurs as this glass window is abruptly covered with dirt from the gravedigger's shovel.

Another formal device Corman uses to great effect is the freeze frame, seen at the end of the precredit sequence as the prematurely buried man is revealed. Often freeze frames are used to capture moments of exuberance, vitality, or poignancy. Since freezing a frame implies the "death" of the event shown as well as its being fixed in memory, such approaches must fail as often as they succeed. Freezing a frame drains the image of a certain vitality, life, even as it tries to capture a moment of pleasure or power. Corman's freezing of an already dead image shows a superior use of this device. Further, his distortion of the image in keeping with the widescreen (Panavision) image deepens its impact as it subjectifies its meaning for Guy, who sees himself in the coffin.

Guy's burial and resurrection give him a new personality. Paralyzed by his obsession with death, his "actual experiencing" of this state by being buried alive frees him to act, to punish those who tormented him in life. This group consists of four people: the two gravediggers who attempt to disinter him for use as a medical specimen for Emily's father, Dr. Gault; the cynical, unpleasant Dr. Gault himself; and Emily. His emergence from the grave gave Corman yet another opportunity for an effective shock cut, and instead of seeing his face or body, we see the sudden terrified look of Sweeny, the graverobber, and Guy's hands thrust suddenly around his throat. His destruction of Dr. Gault, less obliquely shot, has a similar impact. Like the dead frog they experimented with earlier, Dr. Gault is bound with wires and electrocuted. Corman shoots this with Guy full-figure visible on the left side of the screen, and only the shadow of Dr. Gault, tied to a chair, hands twitching like a begging dog, electrocuted. The earlier unpleasant encounters between Guy and Dr. Gault, who "merely experienced great-

er and lesser degrees of tedium," prepares us for this event. Finally,
Guy appears in Emily's bedroom. When she faints he takes her out to
the moors and buries her alive. Corman shoots their "encounter"—
Guy at last above the prone Emily—with the two characters alone on
the moors. Emily's hair, so carefully put up throughout the film, trails
into the edge of the open grave into which Guy pushes her. Screaming,
she lands squarely lodged in the coffin, and Guy shovels dirt across
her face and open mouth. When Miles arrives to try to save her, she
is already dead, and Guy's self-defensive attack on Miles is stopped by
Kate, who, always watching from the sidelines, shoots her brother to
death.

Credit for the film's power must be shared by its screenwriters,
Beaumont and Russell, who had to invent most of the film, since "the
story was not a story at all . . . [but] more like a formal essay on the
disadvantages and general undesirability of being buried alive." Floyd
Crosby's camerawork also shows his typical intelligence in both the
fluid movement and the abundant sharp shock-cutting. Further credit
must go to Ronald Stein's score. Stein was a long-time collaborator of
Corman's, present from the beginning (*Apache Woman, The Day the
World Ended*), whose haunting scores, particularly for *The Last Woman on Earth* and *The Premature Burial*, add distinction to these works.
Daniel Haller's sets express to perfection Corman's obsession with the
world of decadent romanticism, with even nature, reality, represented
by the twisted, dead vegetation and enshrouding fog of the moors. Ray
Milland, usually unfavorably compared to Vincent Price, contributes
strongly to what are probably Corman's two grimmest films: *X—The
Man with the X-Ray Eyes* and *The Premature Burial*.

The Raven

The Raven (1963) came about because, as Corman said, "both Richard Matheson, our writer, and I were getting tired of the stock Poe
pictures." Having experimented on more than a few occasions with a
fusion of humor and horror in both the early thrillers (*Bucket of Blood*)
and, briefly, the Poe series as well ("The Black Cat" episode of *Tales
of Terror*), it was only natural for Corman to expand the series with a
full-length comedy that is the most optimistic, life-affirming of his Poe
films.

The opening image, the marbleized fluids of the credit sequence,
give little clue to the comic nature of *The Raven*. As Erasmus Craven
(Vincent Price) recites the title poem, we see a string of by now familiar
images: ocean waves crashing against the rocks (a more natural version
of the earlier fluids); an enormous fog-enshrouded mansion surrounded
by dead vegetation; and a coffin. But this sober picture is immediately

undercut by our first view of Erasmus: he is "drawing" with his finger a large raven in midair. The film visualizes this creature as a cartoon, which at once gives Erasmus an aura of childishness. Just how far we have come from the epic neurasthenics of *House of Usher* and *The Premature Burial* is indicated in the next shot, when Erasmus rises to close a banging shutter and bumps his head on a telescope. He says, "Ow!" an unthinkable phrase from Usher or Guy Carrell. However, Erasmus does resemble his predecessors in some ways. Like Locke in "Morella" (*Tales of Terror*), he keeps his beloved, supposedly dead wife nearby, in a coffin. Like Nicholas Medina, he lives in a state of abject misery because of her "death." We even see him react with an hysterical scream worthy of Usher at the unexpected touch of his daughter behind him. The same kind of supersensitive masochism that Corman treated seriously in the earlier films is played for laughs in *The Raven*. Like his fellows in this morbid gallery, Erasmus is an artist, but his "creations"—for example, the cartoon raven—are harmless, even juvenile, compared to the hypnotic bleakness of Guy Carrell's painting, "Some Consummations Devoutly to Be Wish'd" or Usher's frightening renderings of his mad, murderous ancestors. The broad nature of his character is brilliantly affirmed during the battle between himself and Scarabus (Boris Karloff) that climaxes the film.

The Raven diverges significantly from the one film it superficially resembles: "The Black Cat" episode of *Tales of Terror*. Whereas the images in the latter episode were equally disturbing and comic, and the ending anything but optimistic (all the principals are dead or doomed), *The Raven* continuously takes the negative icons of the previous films and, in Bevis Hillier's phrase, forces them through a "process of amicization . . . ."[8] The core idea is taking a threatening image and making it "friendly" by changing the context in which we perceive it. Hillier used this concept to account for the postwar appeal of, for example, Japanese furniture and knick-knacks, and of underwater images such as mermaids and submarines. In *The Raven* we see the crucial "descent" into the depths of the house which is normally a movement from the fragile safety of the "upstairs" into an encounter with, experiencing of, death, as here characterized by Erasmus's bumbling silliness and Dr. Bedloe's (Peter Lorre) comic improvisations (he looks around at the dusty cellar and says, "Hard place to keep clean, huh?"). Even where the dreaded/hoped for encounter with the dead does occur—as Erasmus is forced to snip off a few locks of his father's hair to brew a potion to change Dr. Bedloe from raven to man—the initially frightening image gives way to a solicitous one. The film plays with our expectations of horror throughout, but always opts for a humorous or pleasurable response. When Erasmus's dead father—a typically gruesome image—suddenly "awakens" and grabs his son by the

A relaxed moment, following a typical scene of bedlam in The Raven.

throat, Erasmus (and the audience) expects the worst. The father simply says, "Beware"—a warning to his son of possibly dire develop-
ments. In the previous films the dead are not really dead, but simply
waiting to exact revenge on the weak-willed hero. In *The Raven*, a
dead man tries to deflect danger from his son.

Indeed, the film represents a fundamental reversal of the trend established by the previous entries in the series by having the hero move
from a state of continuous disintegration toward the rarest of conditions
in Corman's works: self-actualization. In the earlier films the rotting,
overripe environment reflected the character's own state; in *The Raven*
the plush, elaborate detail of the two mansions—Erasmus's and Scarabus's—acts as an ironic comment on the main character, throwing his
movement toward selfhood into high relief. It is more than a little
significant that the film presents two distinct environments—the two
mansions—since it thus more consciously counterpoints Erasmus's
character with that of Scarabus, and Erasmus's movement toward self-
actualization involves a passage from the seeming safety of his own
house to the definite danger of the other. As in the earlier films, the
collapsing world of the protagonist was threatened by the introduction
of a "normal" agent of destruction from the outside world, so this also

occurs in *The Raven*, except that Erasmus Craven represents both the agent of destruction, and the character whose world—a limited, fragile world characterized by his inability to act, to use his magic powers—is destroyed. The "evil" of Scarabus and his comic decline seem secondary to Erasmus's coming to terms with his own power.

Lest this put too heavy a burden of psychological realism on *The Raven*, we should emphasize that the atmosphere of the film is far more expansive, more fantastic, more indulgently comic than its predecessors. It is hardly accidental that Corman should allow his actors to improvise many of their lines in the only Poe film that shows the possibility of happiness in the world. The sense of relaxed controls is everywhere evident in the film, from, particularly, Dr. Bedloe's relentless sarcasm to what Corman called "the biggest look" of any film in the series.

As the story progresses, Corman and Matheson bring up many potentially threatening images, only to shoot them down to size. Before the trip to Scarabus's mansion, the Craven family servant becomes bewitched. The frightening image of a huge bald ax-wielding "maniac," as Dr. Bedloe calls him, is undercut by Bedloe's nervous assumption of a toreador posture. A similar bewitching of Bedloe's son, Rexford (Jack Nicholson), also proves a temporary episode, characteristic of a film that sees even the "pure evil" of Scarabus undermined by his final position as just another henpecked magician.

The film constantly plays tricks with the audience, particularly with respect to Dr. Bedloe. His very mobile allegiances create much of the film's humor. While Bedloe and Rexford and Erasmus and his daughter Estelle (Olive Sturgess) are tied up in the basement of Scarabus's mansion, Bedloe offers to sacrifice them all: "I don't care what you do to them, just let me go!" When Scarabus says; "Don't you care about your friends?" Bedloe looks bewildered and says, "No, why should I?" The intense sexual imagery we saw in the earlier films becomes another butt for the filmmaker's jokes. During Bedloe's attempts to best Scarabus at magic, he "attacks" Scarabus with a wand. Scarabus makes the wand go limp, and Bedloe, disgusted, says, "You . . . you dirty old man!"

The film's best (and most famous) scene is the duel by magic between Scarabus and Erasmus, the latter fighting not only for himself and his daughter and friends (and perhaps his cuckolding wife, Lenore) but for the triumph of good over evil. Their duel is a dazzling recapitulation of images and themes from the earlier films, a mixture of fantasy, humor, and horror not found elsewhere in Corman's work.

The scene opens with a typical high angle shot of the contestants that cuts to low angle closeups of each participant. The music during the scene picks up the visuals—Erasmus's chair ride through the room is marked by a merry-go-round motif; Scarabus's transformation of a bat into a fan is punctuated by tinny Oriental sounds. There is a distinct pattern behind the "weapons" of illusion each man employs, with Scarabus using far more phallic attacks than Erasmus, in the form of snakes, cannonballs, and lances. Indeed, the most intense attack on Erasmus occurs when Scarabus "becomes" his enemy's father, which suddenly weakens Erasmus, breaks his concentration, and allows Scarabus to "kill" Erasmus by impaling him on a spear. *The Pit and the Pendulum's* convoluted destruction of son by father (Francis Barnard-Nicholas by Nicholas-Sebastian) is reprised in the image of Erasmus's destruction through a violent attack by his "father" in the form of Scarabus. The film's upbeat nature forbids Erasmus's real death, however, and he soon reappears above Scarabus, dropping eggs on the old man's head. The battle reprises the film's theme of "amicization" by having Erasmus transform the attacks of Scarabus into comic, lighter-than-air images. Thus when Scarabus creates a snake around Erasmus's neck, Erasmus turns it into a protective neck scarf. Scarabus's cannonball is returned to him but pops open like a pinata, dropping confetti all over an irritated Scarabus. Scarabus, too, is not without humor during this duel. When Erasmus sends Scarabus a bat, the old man turns it into a Japanese fan which he coyly waves across his face. Erasmus, however, is associated with far more positive, life-affirming imagery than Scarabus, from a group of puppies that were once Scarabus's stone gargoyles to the living white birds released from under his waistcoat.

The character of Lenore (Hazel Court) recalls earlier Poe heroines from Elizabeth Medina to Emily Gault. In most of the films we see a cuckolded husband, and *The Raven* is no exception. When Lenore destroys Erasmus's romantic illusions by telling him he is "still such a bore," there is the usual hint of the woman's departure from the male because of an unsatisfied sexuality. Lenore's departure seems more explainable as a lust for power at being associated with Scarabus, the Grand Master of the Brotherhood of Magicians. However, in *The Raven* (and only here), the male moves from an unfocused dissatisfaction and a tendency toward progressive deterioration toward a position of strength and power. To his defeat of Scarabus can be added his rejection of Lenore to form the series' only picture of the self-actualization of the dissolute Corman/Poe hero.

The Masque of the Red Death

The Masque of the Red Death (1964) differs from its predecessors in being the first of the Poe sequence shot in England, and the first that did not utilize Corman's standard production unit (Daniel Haller as Art Director was the major exception). Corman's successful use of an En-

glish cast and crew and, most notably, Nicolas Roeg in place of Floyd
Crosby, shows both how formalized the conventions of the series had
become—so that others besides the originators of the "Poe look" could
work on the films to much the same end—and by extension how thoroughly the Poe films were a product of Corman's ideas. Roeg's daz-
zlingly mobile camerawork, for example, has clear antecedents in
Crosby's elaborate tracks and dollies in *The Haunted Palace* and *The
Pit and the Pendulum,* while the use of complex color schemes, shock
cuts, and post-production laboratory opticals in *Masque* has earlier
parallels in films like *House of Usher* and *The Premature Burial.*

The Masque of the Red Death is a complex merging of two Poe tales,
the title story, and "Hop-Toad." The first is a typical Poe mood piece,
representing existential anxiety as a bloody plague; the second an
equally typical revenge tale. Even sympathetic students of Corman (for
example, David Pirie in *The Millennic Vision*) have complained that
the grafting is unsuccessful,[9] but *The Masque of the Red Death* is in
many ways Corman's most fully realized, satisfying Poe film. Here the
director moves away from the narrow, enclosed, paranoid vision of
House of Usher and *The Pit and the Pendulum* in favor of a broader,
almost epic approach. *Masque* uncharacteristically contrasts two opposing societies—the suffering villagers and the wealthy revelers in the
castle, rather than focus in on a single small group of people in an
insular environment. Unlike most of its predecessors, *Masque* details
a "real" world outside the enclosed world of the anthropomorphic castle. The opposition of two worlds—the larger, conformist world in harmony with natural law, and the smaller, individual world in violent
opposition to it—forms the basis of all the films in the series, but both
Masque and the following film, *Tomb of Ligeia,* substantiate both
worlds, rather than make the larger world a fantasy or a memory, visualized by unmistakable matte shots or set off from the story proper
by montage, that only triumphs at the end. *Masque* in particular re-
enacts the basic struggle between the worlds of good and evil, within
a framework of religious/existential questioning. Both forces exist precariously in perhaps the most complex character in the series, the ironically named Prince Prospero (Vincent Price).

Corman devised an extremely elaborate mise-en-scène to match his
story of the "evil" Prospero and his attempts to outwit the Red Death
(and death in general) rampaging through medieval Europe. Some of
the motifs are lifted verbatim from Poe: for example, the celebrated
monochrome chambers, one blue, one yellow, etc., that end in Prospero's black and red devil-worshipping room. Others are original visualizations of thematic concerns—for example, the "monks," death's
messengers, who wander through the countryside, each dressed in a
different color. This is unquestionably Corman's most intensely de-

signed film, with the richness of color noted earlier in the series in *The Pit and the Pendulum* and *The Raven* carried to unsettling extremes in *The Masque of the Red Death*. The use of the color red is particularly noteworthy, since it appears only rarely, in association with the important forces in Prospero's life: the two red-haired women—Juliana (Hazel Court), who weds Satan to "secure her position" in the castle, and Francesca (Jane Asher), the naif whom Prospero works diligently to corrupt, but with whom he also falls in love; and the Red Death, the embodiment of human—Prospero's in particular—mortality that he tries desperately to repel.

The story begins in a fog-enshrouded forest in twelfth-century Italy. An old woman gathering firewood encounters a mysterious, hooded figure in red, apparently a monk, who gives her a "sign." He says, "the day of your deliverance is at hand." The ironic symbol of deliverance is a white rose that turns a bloody red as his hand passes over it. The film's subtheme of violation, desecration by touching, is hinted at here, and more fully developed as the film proceeds. The woman's shabby dress and peasant bearing imply it is poverty, perhaps enslavement, from which she and her fellow villagers will be delivered. Her return to the village is followed by the arrival of Prince Prospero, a character hidden in an ornate coach traveling through the countryside. Significantly, we are aware of his existence ("Make way for Prince Prospero!") before we actually see him, just as the protagonists of *The Pit and the Pendulum* and *House of Usher* are hinted at, talked about, before we actually see them. The introduction of Prospero is typically jarring, as a hand yanks open the coach's curtain to reveal the prince.

This early encounter between Prospero and "his" villagers reinforces the film's surface view of his character as an evil, heartless exploiter unconcerned about the serfs who occupy and farm his land, a barren tract threatened by a mysterious plague, the Red Death. The village is characterized by primitive huts and twisted vegetation, and the inhabitants seem to live in abject poverty and ignorance. The film abounds with animal references and motifs, the first of which appears in the initial encounter between Prospero and his villagers. Indeed, the sheer volume of such references gives the film an entire subtext that supports the theme of the subjugation of mankind by a cruel, malevolent Creator by emphasizing the negative aspects of man's animal nature—his ignorance, symbolic inarticulateness, arrested evolution, and enlightenment. Prospero's first words to the villagers are these: "According to my custom, I've come here to thank you for the year's harvest, and to invite you to a feast. . . ." One of the villagers, a young man named Gino (David Weston), replies, "Where you'll throw us the scraps from your table as if we were dogs." "Exactly!" Prospero snaps. "But these dogs have a loud bark and show their teeth. Why?"

The answer to Prospero's question lay in the "sign" given to the old woman by the "holy man" encountered earlier that day. The possibility of deliverance from Prospero's tyranny has given them the strength to talk back to him, a challenge Prospero does not take lightly. When he orders death to Gino, and another objector, Ludovico (Nigel Green), Francesca—Ludovico's daughter and Gino's beloved—begs him for mercy. Prospero again uses animal imagery in his reply to her: "That is not possible. They have defied me. If my hound bites my hand after I have fed and caressed him, should I allow him to go undisciplined?"

Further events in the village demonstrate both the godlike power Prospero assumes, and the powerful threat against him in the form of a plague, the Red Death, that has taken hold. Annoyed by a screaming woman, he decides to see for himself what is wrong. Corman emphasizes the trauma of what Prospero sees with a laboratory optical, an intense, grainy, mobile closeup of the bloody face of the old woman who had received the sign, now writhing in the throes of the Red Death. Prospero quickly masks his horror, orders the coachmen to take Francesca and the two men to his castle, and leaves a final terse order: "Burn the village to the ground."

Prospero begins to emerge as a complex character even in these seemingly narrow early scenes. His obsession with enlightenment, and with the negative nature of salvation, is hinted at when Gino questions why he wants to destroy the village. "This is the day of your deliverance, remember?" Prospero replies. Here and throughout the film Prospero assumes the position, "personality," and demeanor of God, a God he explicitly views as "a deity long dead." He works hard to achieve the kind of inscrutability and random justice associated with a Creator ("God works in mysterious ways," "It's the will of God"). Though he kills many people throughout the film, he tells Francesca this is "a kindness," because he has spared them the Red Death. Though he has his archers shoot a group of villagers outside his battlements, he demands they spare a child. The human assumption of the role of God is more thoroughly worked out in this film than in other, somewhat similar Corman efforts including *X—The Man with the X-Ray Eyes* or *It Conquered the World*.

In many of its conventions, *Masque* falls in line with the other Poe films. The kind of rotting plushness associated with a decadent world, headed by a corrupt aesthete, which we saw in the earlier films is also present here. Likewise we see an "innocent" whose unwilling entry into this world both brings about its destruction, and educates the innocent into the corruption that exists in the world. In *Masque of the Red Death* it is Francesca who fills the place established earlier by Charles Dexter Ward (*The Haunted Palace*), Craven (*The Raven*), and Philip Winthrop (*House of Usher*). The appeal of corruption—which

has overwhelmed the decadent central character—is always danger-
ously present for the innocent characters, and sometimes they suc-
cumb to it entirely like Charles Dexter Ward. In a surprisingly
optimistic reversal of this trend, *Masque* allows Francesca to see within Prospero's character, to fall in love with something positive she sees,
and finally to depart wholly from the now-collapsed environment.

The film is entirely dynamic in its character development, and we
see changes very early in Francesca, particularly. Brought against her
will to Prospero's castle, she fights bitterly against the servants who
wish to wash her in a luxurious bath. Yet, when Prospero tells his mistress, Juliana, to dress her "in one of your finest gowns," Juliana's balk-
ing at this is met surprisingly by Francesca: "You will do as he told
you." Francesca's power to adapt to her environment carries her
through her bizarre adventures in Prospero's castle.

What is the nature of the world Prospero has created in his castle?
A world of revelry, devil-worship, conscious devotion to "evil." Like
the "Christian God" he so frequently invokes, Prospero demands obe-
dience as the price of salvation, in this case salvation from the Red
Death ravaging the countryside. One of Prospero's interests is Satan-
ism, and he has a particular chamber set up for this purpose which
only "the precious few" are allowed to enter. But Prospero is no ordinary devil-worshipper, embracing evil for the sake of evil. It becomes
increasingly clear that he has embraced Satan as a more "realistic" alternative to a Christian God by turns evil or missing entirely. He is a
kind of theoretician of evil, obsessed with the dark side of human nature as a path to enlightenment, having given up—bitterly—on the
concept of a humane Creator. In the black chamber, he delivers the
following speech to Francesca: "Somewhere in the human mind, dear
Francesca, is the key to our existence. . . . Believe? If you believe,
my dear Francesca, you are . . . gullible. Can you look around this
world and believe in the goodness of a God who rules it? Famine,
pestilence, war, disease, death—they rule this world." Prospero's Satanic orientation masks his bitterness at the betrayal of mankind by an
evil God, and by the ultimate punishment that Prospero seeks, above
anything, to avoid: death.

The film's obsession with death is indicated early, during one of the
initial revelry scenes in the castle. When Prospero's companion Alfredo mentions "terror," the word stimulates a speech by Prospero, which
corresponds to those speeches in the earlier Poe films that defined the
downbeat nature of the world: "What is terror? Come. Silence. Listen.
Is it to awaken and hear the passage of time? Or is it the failing beat
of your own heart? Or is it the footsteps of someone who, just a moment before, was in your room?" Prospero delivers a similar speech
that precedes the violent death of Juliana: "Hush. Listen. The passage

of time. The beating of a heart. The footstep of an assassin—destiny!" In both cases Prospero the teacher is offering "lessons" to his "flock," both the desperate (his fellow noblemen and women) and the devoted (Juliana). In both cases the primary enemy is time and the event in which it culminates: death. Corman visualizes both these scenes to perfection, the former by showing with camera askew a closeup of the peculiar clock in the great hall of Prospero's castle, a clock whose pendulum takes the form of a scythe; the latter by a deep focus shot of the same pendulum swinging in closeup, with Juliana walking slowly forward in the frame, from long-shot to closeup. Thus Corman emphasizes visually his theme of the dominance of time/death over the weak, faltering human personality.

Prospero's ideas about mankind center on their weak, animallike nature. As one of his "jests," he orders his guests to "show me the lives and loves of the animals" by behaving like them. To one guest he says, "How like a pig you are. Be one." To another he says, "How small and insignificant you are, like a worm. Be one." These "entertainments" serve various purposes for Prospero: they reinforce his position above the rabble, his godlike status, since he is proving how backward, ignorant, unevolved people are by making them act like animals; and they provide a "lesson" for Francesca in the sordidness of life, allowing Prospero to remake her "in his own image."

Another lesson for Francesca appears shortly after, when Prospero shows her a falcon killing another bird. Again, Prospero gives a speech that reveals the double nature of his personality—on the one hand, his tyrannical cruelty, on the other his bitterness with life: "Do you know how a falcon is trained, my dear? Her eyes are sewn shut. Blinded, temporarily, she suffers the whims of her god, patiently, until her will is submerged and she learns to serve, as your God has taught and blinded you with crosses." Prospero's use of the phrase "my dear" is not a mere formality, for he appears to be falling in love with Francesca. This scene is particularly noteworthy because it is shot entirely outdoors, with a sense of openness and optimism immediately undercut by the activity we see—the destruction of a bird in flight by the trained falcon. This metaphorical substructure of the film is relentlessly hammered at, the comparisons between mankind and animal revealing at once Prospero's bleak view of humankind and his own need for salvation.

The idea of "whims" reappears in the next scene as an old friend of Prospero's, Scarlatti, arrives at the castle and begs entry. Rebuffed, Scarlatti says, "Prospero, I know your *whims*, but . . . ," whereupon Prospero informs him of the presence of the Red Death and by implication, his possible contamination, and shoots him in the neck: "For you, friend," he says. This verbal link between scenes reinforces Pros-

pero's assumption of the role of God in the absence of a real one, and
shows how much he resembles the Christian God he despises: instead
of meting out justice in a moral or ethical fashion, he does it with a
certain amount of randomness and unpredictability. In the scene in
which he has Gino and Ludovico fight, during which Ludovico is killed
by Prospero in front of Francesca, Gino calls the Prince "a madman,"
to which the latter replies, "And yet I shall live and you will die." This
is another of Prospero's reminders of the absence of humanity or mercy
in life.

Francesca's change in personality is not entirely clear until her last
scene with Prospero, but other characters move more quickly toward
their destiny. Her father is killed by Prospero, and Gino "set free" by
the prince to die with the Red Death. Juliana undergoes "the most
terrible rites and incantations" in order to marry the Devil, to secure
her position of favor in Prospero's eyes. In a striking montage, Corman
visualizes this "ceremony" in wildly archetypal/Freudian terms, with
Juliana prone in a dreamy, foggy landscape, menaced by a variety of
oddly dressed characters all of whom carry a cutting weapon that they
use on her. Her screams and agonized expressions result from a symbolic castration performed by these characters, who incarnate the
film's themes of time and death (one resembles Father Time, with a
scythe). Shortly after this montage, Juliana is brutally murdered, paid
back by Prospero for her attempt to get Francesca out of the castle and
out of the Prince's sight.

The film's modified optimism, which requires the death of the corrupt Juliana, allows for the salvation of Gino and Francesca. Gino's
expulsion from the castle is traced in a dizzying series of mobile shots
that refrain a similar, earlier scene of Francesca, tormented and confused, running through the castle. The change in Gino is confirmed
during his talk with a holy man (in reality, a representative of the Red
Death) in which Gino admits, "I'm afraid, I'm afraid!" This admission
of weakness contrasts with his earlier arrogance in dealing with Prospero, and seems to assure his salvation.

Francesca's fascination with the castle and its luxury—particularly
evident in her enchantment with the monochrome rooms through
which Prospero leads her shortly after her arrival—gives way to a fascination with Prospero himself. His solicitousness for her is counterpointed by brutal acts against her father, lover, and all those around
them, but Prospero does appear to win her over. During their final
parting after the arrival of the "Red Death" (dressed as a monk), Francesca says, "My life is done. The rest I give to you." Instructed by the
holy man to wait by the battlements (for Gino), she kisses Prospero
good-bye, and looks at him with lingering sadness, unquestionably in

The dance of death in Masque of the Red Death.

love with him. Prospero, too, appears to feel this emotion, as we see a kind of wounded quality not noted previously in him.

The film culminates in a lurid "dance of death" that almost justifies claims of plagiarism by Corman from Bergman's *The Seventh Seal,* though the similarities are only superficial. In the Bergman film the use of visual absolutes—black and white—lacks any real feeling of decadence, and loses the sense of individual, human entrapment in its rather abstract tableau. Corman's blood-spattered group, gathered around and clawing at Prospero, shown in closeup and long-shot and for a much longer time than Bergman's masochistic trio, jerkily acts out the film's theme of suffering humanity, dancing like puppets to the tune of an evil God. Corman also uses this scene to reinforce other ideas contained in the film, for example, the horror of touching. Throughout the film Prospero was literally untouchable, often shot above the rabble, either on the battlements or on one of the staircases from which he threw diamonds to his "greedy" friends. During the dance, the diseased, dying revelers drown him in a sea of hands and bodies, their allegiance switched from Prospero to Death.

This climactic scene has also been criticized, by Corman devotees like David Pirie, as "very near to being an embarrassing failure,"[10] the objection being more in the execution of the scene than in the idea of it. However, the very luridness that Pirie objects to can be seen as a virtue in light of the film's overall design. The music is extremely somber, primarily a sparingly used drum and tambourine, and the movements of the people, whom we have seen in varius dehumanized states throughout the film, appropriately stylized. The most important aspect of the scene is the presence of Prospero in the midst of it, trapped by those he had manipulated earlier, and finally abandoned entirely as they fall one by one, dead at his feet. The details of choreography do not seem important, since we are dealing simply with puppetlike characters, manipulated in life and death.

A more serious objection to the film is its faulty integration of the Hop-Toad story into what is basically an existential melodrama. Certainly there are many superficial links between the scene of the dwarf's revenge against Alfredo, his dressing of this character in an ape suit for the Masque, then setting him on fire. Pirie has commented on how, "in relation to Poe's psychological constellation, it can be seen as the revolt of the son against father."[11] The Hop-Toad scenes relate also to the substructure of animal motifs in the film, with Alfredo's reversion-to-type (the cruel, stupid ape) the necessary precedent for his destruction. But there is little doubt that, in spite of the effectiveness of the episode in itself, it bears no relation to the story as a whole and seems to detract from the tale of one man's vain attempt to replace the modern, missing God with himself.

The Tomb of Ligeia

The precredit sequence of Corman's last Poe film hints at a continuation of the theme of *Masque of the Red Death*—the portrayal of a doomed challenger to God's natural laws. Again we see a spiritually disenchanted male, Verden Fell (Vincent Price), burying his supposedly dead wife. Attendants to this burial argue with Fell that his wife, Ligeia, has no right being "buried in consecrated ground." The reason? "She was not a Christian!" Fell reminds them, "This is my ground," to which one of them replies, "It is the Lord's ground." Fell has the final word in the following blasphemy: "Then let the Lord refuse her."

This initial view of the film as a perhaps typical Corman-Poe rendering of the hubris-ridden questioner attempting to destroy or avert natural law (death) is undercut even as it unravels. First, this opening sequence is shot in the true outdoors—the English countryside—and not in what Corman has called the "claustrophobic, insular world of the older films." This opening of the world of the film into the world of reality immediately lends credence to Corman's stated view of the film as, uncharacteristically, a "love story," an opinion shared by its writer, Robert Towne. Indeed, Towne's participation in the project coincided with Corman's desire "to experiment on this picture" to make *The Tomb of Ligeia* (1964) by far the most unconventional entry in the series, a film that diverges significantly from the tone and technique of the earlier works.

Corman has expressed two contradictory opinions about the film: on the one hand calling it perhaps his favorite of the series; on the other criticizing it for its most distinctive quality, its openness: "[I filmed] a fair amount of the picture in the English countryside . . . I shot a great deal in natural sunlight. As a result, the picture has a bigger look, but I still think my original theory and practice were the most effective."[12] This openness is largely due to Towne's script, which incorporates much of the Corman-Poe iconography—false deaths, personality transference, and disintegration, rerenderings of the human form as art (paintings or waxen images)—in the context of a surprisingly hopeful, by turns violent and tender love story. *Masque of the Red Death's* linking of religious challenge with a denial of death (since God represents the ultimate given in the universe), becomes secondary in this story of the attempts by Rowena (Elizabeth Shepherd) to break Ligeia's posthumous hold on Verden, the man she loves.

Towne's earlier collaboration with Corman, *The Last Woman on Earth* (1960), began with a ruthless cockfight in Puerto Rico, and *The Tomb of Ligeia* contains a similar scene that establishes the kind of universe in which the film operates. A fox hunt is in progress, an event Corman shoots in the real outdoors, with hand-held camera, a technique that would have been unthinkable in *House of Usher* or *The Premature Burial*. This "sporting" activity, merely a diversion for the members of the gentry who indulge in it, is seen as ruthlessly unfair, introducing a view of mankind as—like the fox—utterly victimized by "higher forces." This generalized metaphor becomes more specific as Rowena, never very interested in the fox hunt, departs from the group, an irritating "willful" act noted by her father and her friend Christopher (John Westbrook) who is also in love with her. Rowena's divergence from the group shows her rejection of its cruelty, and, indeed, Rowena emerges quickly as a complex woman, alternately intrigued and repelled by "evil."

Rowena rides through a ruined abbey of spectacular beauty, stopping at the grave we saw in the opening sequence. This passage from her peers into the abbey and what it represents links Rowena with earlier life-affirming characters in the series (Philip Winthrop in *House of Usher*, Francis Barnard in *The Pit and the Pendulum*) who enter a static, dead world in order to destroy it. Corman's self-consciously vis-

ual treatment of this passage—slow pans and tracks—gives the movement the mythic resonance that marks it as the first step in a primal
battle between past and present, evil and good. Most of the shots here
begin as static compositions, but immediately begin panning to left or
right, Corman thereby imbuing the dead environment of the abbey
with a kind of life which, as we will see, depends for its existence
entirely on Verden Fell's tormented consciousness.

Corman renders much of the film with extremely stylized camerawork, a strategy of artistic self-consciousness meant, perhaps, to "make
up for" the fact that the film is shot largely outdoors. The first encounter between Rowena and Verden provides a case in point. A graceful
track follows Rowena as she rides into the ruin; this track ends with
the camera behind her, an over-the-shoulder point of view shot that
rises slightly as she sees Ligeia's grave—on top of which a black cat
sits. As Rowena articulates the name on the grave—"Ligeia"—the cat
leaps on her, causing her to fall onto the flower-covered grave. Corman
shoots this fall for maximum traumatic effect, in a series of jarring quick
cuts. Rowena's toughness is indicated as she raises herself and smiles
at the cat, but Corman hints at the struggle for dominance between
the two women—one alive, one dead—by framing this encounter in
high/low angle cuts, the cat looking down, Rowena looking up. Rowena
is thus literally "brought down" by Ligeia embodied in the cat, the first
of many savage encounters between the two.

In previous Poe films, Corman often introduced his troubled protagonists with a radical camera movement, at a quiet moment just after
a previous trauma. *The Tomb of Ligeia* follows this strategy as Rowena
stands on the grave and reaches, with a friendly gesture, for the cat.
An abrupt cut shows Verden entering the frame from the left, the camera positioned at a low angle, followed immediately with a radically
quick zoom into his face and Rowena's scream. Such extreme techniques in what is after all the simple introduction of a character show
the extreme, over-the-edge qualities of a man like Verden, and hint at
the struggle that must take place between Rowena and Verden/Ligeia.

Verden refuses to deal with "reality," a fact immediately clear from
the presence of powerful sunglasses—"a morbid reaction to sunlight,"
he says. His creation of, and retreat into, a world of his own devising
is progressively detailed. We learn he is an artist, well-versed in creating wax effigies that strongly resemble real people. A troubled figure,
he haunts his own abbey, preferring to move among past, dead, de-
composing things than to adjust to Ligeia's death and live. Rowena's
arrival on the scene is both desired and feared by Verden, who can
either continue to sink into his own inert world, or move beyond it.

Rowena emerges as a strong, even reckless woman—like Ligeia she
is criticized by her father for being "willful" (a word that appears fre-

quently in the film). Like Verden she, too, is in some ways an extreme character, intensely curious about Verden's odd image and attitude, even willing to embrace his morbidness fully as she puts one of his "flowers of death" into her lapel and smiles. Yet even as she embraces, she challenges. As he is carrying her toward his house (she has twisted her ankle, it seems), she suddenly tears off his glasses, inducing a traumatic reaction in the overcivilized Verden. But he too is becoming less predictable. In spite of this act he does not reject her. He picks her up again and continues to carry her.

The romantic aspects of the film become apparent during Verden's carrying of Rowena toward the house. There is a sense of relaxation in the visuals here, as the shots switch freely from mobile point of view shots of Rowena observing the ruins around them, long shots of the two dwarfed by the massive collapsing walls and archways, and close-ups of the two of them. The film's theme of primal conflict between self-destruction and self-creation is hardly evident here as the successful merging of two opposing sensibilities—the joining of the separated, lost aspects of a single personality—appears to begin.

As so often in Corman's films, we have again in *The Tomb of Ligeia* the problem of vision, of "seeing." Our first postcredits view of Verden shows the most direct link to his mind—the "window to the soul," the eyes—hidden behind thick sunglasses. During a conversation with Rowena, Verden chides her on her "limited" vision:

ROWENA: Do you ever laugh, Mr. Fell?

VERDEN: Only at myself.

ROWENA: I see.

VERDEN: Do you? You keep saying, "I see," but I think your vision is even more limited than mine.

Verden views Rowena as a kind of innocent, unaware of the world's horrors. Unlike him, however, she exists as a conscious member of the outer world, the world from which he turns away. Her attempts to bring him into the world, to remove once and forever his sunglasses, and his complex strategies in fighting her, form the basis of the film.

The violence of their relationship, hinted at during their first meeting, reaches a deeper level when Rowena arrives unannounced to deliver a note from Christopher. This innocent act triggers Verden's rage, and Corman visualizes this with an extraordinary combination of static framing and point of view forward/backward dollies. Rowena's passage from the bright countryside into Verden's gloomy mansion is doubly emphasized by Corman shooting her in long shot, standing like a statue at one end of the main room, her face and figure almost completely covered by shadows. Verden, disturbed from his reverie, rises and walks menacingly toward her, and the camera here alternates between point of view shots of Verden observing and moving excitedly toward the frozen Rowena, and forward dollies of Verden, the last shot rising slightly above Rowena as Verden descends to strangle her. Rowena's understanding of the basic parameters of the relationship becomes apparent as she saves herself by removing his glasses, an act which immediately confuses Verden, throwing him out of his inner world into the real one. This violent encounter, typically, precedes a loving caress.

Rowena's attraction to Verden contrasts with her lack of enthusiasm for the more ostensibly suitable mate, Christopher. His world, she says, is "law and logic . . . to be so limited!" (Significantly, she uses Verden's word describing her, in reference to Christopher.) Rowena's attraction to Verden indicates her desire to encounter a dangerous, spiritual world, the world of "the other" created by Verden as a more acceptable alternative to the "limited" real world. At the same time, both the melodramatic model and Corman's own films show that this merging of an individualized, dying world, a world of self-destruction, with the "real" world of self-creation, cannot be successful, and must end with the triumph of one or the other.

Corman traces this attempt by Rowena to merge with/destroy Verden's world during one of the film's two major set-pieces, the luring of Rowena into the bell-tower by the cat. Corman's attitudes are too individualized to permit a strong case for his influencing by other directors, but the parallels between this scene and Hitchcock's *Vertigo* are striking and must be commented on. In both films we see two women, one of them spiritual and "dead," the other a more sensual and earthy living counterpart. This unreal and real pair is played in both films by the same actress, and in both cases the question of true mortality is raised. In both films a traumatized male character stands as a kind of weak link between them. The scene in the bell tower in *The Tomb of Ligeia*, though employed for entirely different purposes than similar scenes in *Vertigo*, clinches the resemblance. In both cases this locale is exploited for its symbolic value—the bell-tower is part of a church or abbey, with the salvation or destruction of the personality the two possibilities for the character who finds him/herself there. (The bell itself acts as a double symbol of civilization/cultural values— marriage—and natural law—time and death—in its inevitable movements.)

However, *Ligeia's* resemblance to *Vertigo* can be ultimately traced almost entirely to Towne's script—to characters and settings rather than actors or visuals. Corman's visualization of the film in general and the bell-tower scene specifically does not derive from Hitchcock, and a close reading of the sequence will bear this out.

This is a complexly structured segment, with several levels of consciousness operating at once. Rowena is inside the house, while Verden and Christopher have decided to take a walk through the abbey
to look at Ligeia's grave. We see fleeting glimpses of the two men talking, but we hear Verden's speech throughout this lengthy scene. What
we see is, primarily, Rowena's attempt to retrieve a pair of glasses from
the cat, who has worked them onto its head somehow and is luring her
away from the house and into the bell-tower. Verden's speech begins
with his remembrances of Ligeia's physical deterioration; onscreen we
see the cat taking the glasses and Rowena following it. Verden says,
"She seemed to turn to the very stones of the abbey for renewed
strength!" and we see Rowena touching the same rotting stones, wend-
ing her way *up*. (This is a significant reversal in itself, since in the
previous Poe films, it was the passage *down*, into the family crypts,
that led to the confrontation of personality and death, a convention
Towne's more hopeful film turns around.) Ligeia's fervent wish "only
for life!" contrasts with Rowena's movement toward her own death, the
deathlike ambience of Verden's beloved bell-tower. Ligeia's presence
in the abbey was powerful, according to Verden: "Ligeia *became* the
abbey . . . she never entered or left a room, never went down the dark
passageway without somehow illuminating it like a single moving can-
dle." Rowena, too, moves through the passageway, but controlled, almost unwilling, led along by the cat/Ligeia/Verden. Corman shoots
these movements as a series of rapid cuts, with stark low angle framing,
Rowena trapped by the dark stone, and the wooden superstructure
that holds the bell. She moves far up into the bell-tower, and eventually becomes trapped as the cat leaps deftly onto the bell, then onto
the other side. Corman cuts to Verden talking about his fear of being
"insane," carving off the date of Ligeia's death and not realizing it until
that moment, when he sees marble dust on his hands. His anguish is
interrupted by the "alarming" sounds of the tolling bell, at which point
he and Christopher run to the tower to save Rowena, who is screaming
hysterically and holding her ears.

Corman's framing of this entire scene within Verden's voiceover indicates Verden's control, even creation of what is occurring. Though
various characters talk frequently of the "willfulness" of both Ligeia
and Rowena, it is Verden's will and power that have in some sense
seduced Rowena out of the natural, normal world and into his disintegrating one. Rowena's subjugation by the cat/Ligeia is also Verden's
attempt to "break" her, to absorb her personality into his just as he
tried to strangle her earlier in the film. Like Corman, Verden stands
outside the scene, a godlike "narrator" talking of nothing but death
and destruction, yet creating it, breathing life into it as he talks. This
scene separates Corman's approach from Hitchcock's, where *Vertigo's*

Scotty (James Stewart) is much more the victim than the creator of the "other" world than the troubled but participating, inventing Verden Fell.

Corman cuts from Rowena's entrapment, near-death, to her marriage to Verden, both events accompanied aurally by the tolling of bells. Again we see the love story aspect of the film during the honeymoon montage. In a voiceover, both Verden and Rowena talk about their childhood, and Corman illustrates this simple conversation with extreme long shots of the two walking along the beach and through a field of flowers, suggesting their attunement to nature, their relaxation with natural forces. Verden, most significantly, has abandoned his glasses. They visit Stonehenge, and compare it with the abbey, giving a sense of timelessness to their love: both, says Verden, have "a sense of purpose." This open, pleasurable encounter is self-consciously framed inside a sort of oblong iris, with the screen space around the iris black, indicating the fleeting, artificial nature of the moment between them. This is reinforced when they return to the abbey, and Rowena observes Verden putting on his dark glasses.

The framing of shots from inside fireplaces—a frequent strategy in the Poe films—reaches its apex in *The Tomb of Ligeia*. Fire itself is a common enough symbol, with ritual purgation of the dying world of Roderick Usher characterized by flaming destruction. But a fireplace represents something different—the tentative, temporary control of nature. Corman uses it more specifically to undercut verbal messages of complex or deceitful characters. At the beginning of the mesmerism sequence in *The Tomb of Ligeia*, Rowena chides Verden about "disappearing" the previous night. Verden replies, "You had best come to me, my dear. I never left my room," and Corman frames this shot from inside the fireplace, with the flames flickering along the bottom of the frame, signaling Verden is lying. Verden's lie takes on added weight as Corman cuts to a closeup of Rowena, with the flames now much larger than before, almost obliterating her face as he attempts to mesmerize her: "No harm, no harm will come to you . . . give over your will to mine." The absorption of Rowena's personality into Verden's (also into Ligeia's, with whose voice she will speak) is rendered in these fireplace shots, with the flames larger than her face. As she sinks into a hypnotic state, the camera tracks slightly forward into a tighter closeup, then cuts to a medium shot of the room, incorporating the now-hypnotized Rowena, her manipulator Verden, and the flames flickering along the bottom of the frame. Thus the environment is reborn. Rowena's world is re-created as Verden's.

Verden's demonstration is not intended to show the unbelievers (their dinner guests) that mesmerism exists, but to open the way for the supplanting of Rowena's strong but vulnerable personality with

Ligeia's. He recasts her into the most vulnerable personality, that of a child, has her chase an imaginary butterfly, entreats her not to cry when it flies away. But Rowena suddenly assumes a third identity during a childhood song. As she sings, she stops on the words, "I *will*. . . ." The camera tracks into closeup and her expression changes to a hard, seemingly conscious stare and she articulates Ligeia's last words, adapted from Joseph Glanville: "will? . . . will! . . . Who knoweth the mysteries of the will? The will herein lies that dieth not. Man need not kneel before the angels nor lie in death forever, but for the weakness of his feeble will. I will always be your wife!" At this point, Rowena faints.

This is an important speech, perhaps the closest Corman comes in *The Tomb of Ligeia* to a self-contained verbal articulation of the world inhabited by the Corman/Poe "hero." Yet the speech comes not from Verden, but from his dead wife through his living one, another radical difference between this film and the previous ones. If we see Verden, however, as the controlling force behind Ligeia, this speech must also express his personality. The film offers continuous evidence that Verden's is the consciousness that pervades the film, not Ligeia's, that it is Verden rather than Ligeia who is behind the mysterious "attacks" on Rowena in the form of the black cat, Ligeia's black hairs in Rowena's hairbrush. The film plays a fairly typical cat-and-mouse game with the audience about whether Verden is responsible for what is happening. In this way, *The Tomb of Ligeia* resembles *The Pit and the Pendulum*, where Nicholas Medina's "definite air of guilt" points to that character as another simultaneously weak and controlling personality. Like Medina, the masochistic Verden blames himself for what is happening— for example, the chipping away of the date of Ligeia's death—at the same time he portrays himself as a victim. This self-blame not only validates the collapse of the personality, but moves the entire film away from "spiritual hocus-pocus" into the realm of psychological drama. (Indeed, the one Poe film with the most unmistakable and clear-cut fantasy elements is also the most optimistic of the group: *The Raven*. The horrific and fantastic elements of the Poe films can be explained primarily as the acting-out of the self-destructive desires of the protagonists, and *The Raven* is the only one of the films that features a life-affirming character.)

The long-awaited resurrection of the possibly dead typically occurs toward the end of the Poe films as a climactic event that triggers the disintegration of the "hero." Not surprisingly, the "body" in Ligeia's tomb is a wax effigy, lovingly created by Verden; the "real" Ligeia is preserved in Verden's work chamber, lying on a canopied bed with arms outstretched in death. It is typical of these overcivilized Poe characters to populate their worlds with dead likenesses of people (Verden's

Egyptian sarcophagus heads) as well as with actual dead people. This
represents a denial of death—an at least temporary resolution of the
fear of death—and the artist's desire to reshape the world—unwieldy,
self-motivated, selfish, or unloving human personality—to his own
specifications.

The chamber in which Verden works is not only the location of the
real, dead Ligeia, it is also Verden's ultimate psychic zone, which the
persistent Rowena finally breaks into. Corman emphasizes the "otherness" of this environment not only with surveying shots of the stat-
uary and anthropomorphic shapes created by Verden, but also with
many tilted and fireplace shots. This lengthy climax is the film's crucial
scene, the final encounter between the life-affirming Rowena, the
death-obsessed Verden, and the "dead-but-alive" Ligeia. Rowena's
force is pitted against two forces, the merging of Ligeia and Verden
already having occurred, as we note from Verden's controlled, zombie-
like behavior. The attack on Rowena is made explicit as she discovers
the dead form of Ligeia and falls "accidentally" into her arms, a deadly
embrace recalling earlier, seemingly unwilling couplings of living and
dead in *House of Usher* and *Tales of Terror*. Rowena's entrapment is
beautifully expanded as a black moire netting falls onto the two women
and Rowena, screaming, struggles to free herself.

Verden's servant, Kenrick, reveals his master's secret: Ligeia hyp-
notized Verden on her deathbed, "she held him with her eyes," and
forced him to "care for her" even after death, to resurrect her body
and replace it with a wax alternative, so that "I will always be your
wife." Rowena's subsequent assumption of Ligeia's identity for a "good"
purpose—to free Verden from the bondage of posthypnotic, posthumous control—is another aspect of the film without parallel in the series, and further evidence of Towne's selective use of the genre
conventions established by Corman. This strategy seems to backfire as
Rowena's speech in which she pretends to be Ligeia and says, "I am
dying," ends with Rowena's apparent death. As in *The Pit and the Pendulum*, the "game" of assuming another's identity becomes too real as
the original personality is destroyed by the assumed one—an important indicator of Corman's view of the essential weakness and mutability of the human mind.

This final sequence is among Corman's most complex set-pieces,
with the Rowena-Ligeia identities shifting wildly in the chaotic, fiery
environment of the chamber. Rowena's apparent sacrifice to free Verden by "becoming" the dead Ligeia allows Verden to throw Ligeia's
body into the fire. Yet "Ligeia" reappears as the black cat, crouching
on the "dead" Rowena's prone body. Verden knocks the creature off,
and while it lies insensate, Rowena appears to stir back to life. When
the cat awakes, Rowena again appears dead. After Verden leaves her

Tomb of Ligeia: *(top) Verden Fell's world collapses; (bottom) The entrapment of personality during the "accidental" embrace between the dead Ligeia and the living Rowena.*

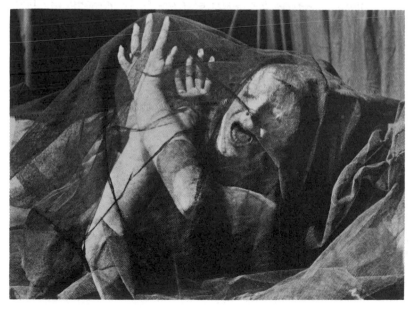

bed in confusion and despair, he looks back across the chamber to see
a gauze-enshrouded figure walking toward him. Corman renders this
resurrection in reverse matching shots of Verden, then the woman, the
first tilted left, the second tilted right. Verden's hopeful anticipation of
Rowena is broken as she lifts the veil and reveals herself as a laughing
Ligeia. He leaps on her and strangles her as she laughs at him. These
shots are rendered in agitated closeups, often through the flames of
the open fires Verden has burning throughout the chamber. Corman
reiterates the idea of Verden as the creator of all that is happening, by
contrasting the visual message—that the woman is Ligeia—with what
we learn shortly after—that it was Rowena. Corman shoots the scene
primarily from Verden's viewpoint; because he *thinks* he is strangling
Ligeia, the woman we *see* is Ligeia. Verden's confusion increases when
he realizes he has murdered—"again!"—Rowena. Rowena's "double
death" recalls the two deaths—like Rowena's, both false—of Elizabeth
Medina in *The Pit and the Pendulum.*

   The destruction of Verden and his environment begins in earnest
after Christopher removes Rowena's body from the chamber. This
leaves Verden alone with the cat, which leaps onto his face and scratch-
es out his eyes. Verden's blind staggerings, his eyes bleeding, cause
him to accidentally set the chamber on fire, and in the midst of the
destruction, Verden finally murders the cat/Ligeia, then dies himself.
The true deaths of Verden and Ligeia—the latter now in human form—
trigger Rowena's rebirth, in the optimistic last shot of the film.

6

Critical Reactions

CORMAN'S CRITICAL ACCEPTANCE has been stronger abroad than in his own country, with British and French critics typically more willing to accept his dehumanized, annihilating worldview as the credible vision of an original artist.

Like other directors who have offered audiences a narrow, bleak view of life, Corman has had a preponderantly negative American press. While the mass audience has responded to his films to the extent of making him a multimillionaire and a virtual household word, his insistence on featuring such apparently unpleasant topics as violent criminality (*The St. Valentine's Day Massacre*), incest and homosexuality (*Bloody Mama*), drugs (*The Trip*), and rape (*The Wild Angels*) has alienated critics who prefer to see portrayed the world they experience, which is perhaps far from the disenfranchised group of Hell's Angels, drug addicts, neurasthenics, and criminals who populate many of Corman's films. The Poe series has received the most positive reaction, unsurprising considering their plush trappings, desirable source material, "decent actors" like Vincent Price and Boris Karloff, and heavy air of internalization. These qualities have somewhat obscured the utterly despairing view of life works like *The Masque of the Red Death* and *The Pit and the Pendulum* share with their more socially conscious counterparts.

The first Corman film even reviewed in the *New York Times* was *The House of Usher* in 1960. However, the *Times* usually ignored low-budget efforts during the 1950s, unless they featured well-known actors or came out of a major studio. *Variety* operated under more egalitarian rules, concerning itself more with marketing possibilities than aesthetics, and most of Corman's films from that decade are reviewed in its pages. Since the paper tended to admire works that might be successful, Corman's films received relatively good reviews, with the notable exception of *Teenage Doll*, a key 1950s film that *Variety* moralistically panned.

The Poe films, a groundbreaking series for Corman in so many ways, also brought him the acclaim that had eluded him in his early days as

Corman's most famous creation: Vincent Price as Roderick Usher in the Poe series, framed by the elegant objects of his self-created world.

a director. Of course, he had a reputation as a fast, efficient, colorful filmmaker throughout the 1950s, but nobody took the films seriously. With *The House of Usher,* articles began appearing, and Corman became associated with something other than "mere" low-budget films. The Poe series received both critical and commercial acclaim in England, where two of the films were shot. *Films and Filming* devoted spreads to most of the series, although the otherwise progressive *Movie* had little to say about Corman. This situation was repeated in France, where the commercial press received Corman enthusiastically, while auteurist magazines like *Positif* showed minimal awareness of the director. The French Film Institute held the first retrospective of Corman's work in 1964.

In America, Corman's defenders throughout the key decade of the 1960s, when his reputation was solidified, could be found primarily in some quarters of the commercial press and in the fan magazines. The earliest significant critical attention came to his films from what were essentially elaborate "fanzines" like *Famous Monsters of Filmland* and, most important, Calvin Beck's landmark *Castle of Frankenstein.* It may appear far-fetched to claim that either of these magazines, aimed at a young audience, was even capable of "significant" criticism, but they were both essential in creating and nurturing the Corman legend. These magazines reviewed scores of Corman films for new generations of filmgoers, engaged in lengthy debates on the relative merits of the films, and published interviews. They stimulated the growth of "Shock Theater" television matinees which featured films like *Attack of the Crab Monsters* and *It Conquered the World* long after their original release. One issue of *Castle of Frankenstein* contained a six-page pure plot description of *Not of this Earth.* Some of the writers for these magazines—for example, Jon Davidson (now a prominent producer) and Joe Dante (director)—parlayed personal obsessions with Corman into careers with him.

The early and mid-1960s was a period of revisionism for film students and scholars. After the French "rediscovered" the American commercial cinema, their American counterparts, led by *Film Culture*'s critic Andrew Sarris, picked up the lead. In ranking directors under such exotic categories as "Expressive Esoterica" and "Strained Seriousness," Sarris was merely recapitulating *Cahiers du Cinema*'s "politique des auteurs." But it was a concept—director as artist and creator—America was ready for. Film societies and revival houses began to investigate America's exceedingly rich film past, and the term "commercial" was not only no longer anathema, but to some extent even a plus in resurrecting works by previously dismissed "hacks" like Samuel Fuller, Edgar G. Ulmer, and Joseph H. Lewis.

One might have supposed Corman would fall into place with the other auteurs, particularly when we consider that one of the earmarks of an "auteur" (though by no means necessary to that status) was control of a film in both production and direction. While he never wrote his own scripts (only "tampering" with them to various degrees), Corman was the independent producer-director par excellence, financing the films, developing a stock company both before and behind the camera, and "interfering" with the script and the editing. But auteurists have argued that control can exist in a vacuum, citing a director like Hugo Haas as an auteur "devoid of personal style" and with "nothing to say." Most critics have consigned Corman to this state, with the main barrier being the "rarely memorable acting," as Georges Sadoul phrased it, a virtual *sine qua non* of Corman's films. Rarely has an attempt been made to factor in the "bad acting" as a complex amalgam of Corman's intimidation by actors, his fear of accepting *in toto* the Godlike role of the director, and his use of actors as blanks or ciphers inhabiting a world of utter pointlessness.

Two books devoted entirely to Corman's career have appeared in recent years: Ed Naha's *Brilliance on a Budget* and *The Movie World of Roger Corman*, edited by Philip di Franco. Neither book has much critical value, but both are useful for the abundance of interviews with Corman and his associates. Both books employ a slapdash style and both give clear indications of Corman's status as a phenomenon (historical) rather than an artist (aesthetic), by concentrating, like Corman himself, on quantity: how many films he made, how quickly he made them, how many of his protégés outstripped Corman in fame, how much money he saved by filming back to back, and so on.

Prior to these books, which constitute almost the entire shelf on Corman in English, the Edinburgh Film Festival published a now infamous monograph on Corman to supplement a retrospective of his work held in 1971. The book, a compilation of essays by Paul Willeman, David Will, David Pirie, and Lynda Myles, covers a variety of topics pertaining to the films. Titled *Roger Corman: The Millennic Vision*, the book was one of a series that also covered Jacques Tourneur, Douglas Sirk, Raoul Walsh, and Frank Tashlin. The entire series gained a certain notoriety among anti-intellectual and antiauteurist critics as examples of the extremes to which auteurists would go in ferreting out "themes" and "visual style" in directors whose acceptance as artists was hardly universal. The Corman book was considered the crown jewel in this paste tiara, with Bill Warren's judgment that the book was "the most overintellectualized flapdoodle that has ever been devoted to a director of cheap monster movies"[1] perhaps a definitive indicator of the book's general reception.

Dumbfounded critical reaction, however, should not obscure the brilliant insights the book has to offer on Corman. In attempting to be particularly polemical—a not unreasonable approach considering Corman's poor reputation—some of the essays go to great lengths to justify the director by citing anthropological tracts, ontological concepts like "sacred and profane time" and the much-remarked "phallic trickster," and phenomenology. Such an approach obviously derives from the authors' academic background, a fact hammered home by the presence of elaborate charts showing the cyclical approach to time in Corman's films.

But beyond the charts and the polysyllabic words, *The Millennic Vision* contains by far the best criticism of Corman in English. Paul Willeman's introductory essay is particularly valuable, a model of compressed insight. Willeman divides the films into groups depicting "the birth of a new society," "the period leading up to the millennium," "a complete cycle in Time," and "efforts to escape from the eternal cycle." Willeman's structuring of the films into these categories allows him to deal profoundly with the distinct elements that comprise the films, for example, the dominant woman, the Freudian aspects, the preponderance of destroyed societies, and so on. Willeman also analyzes Corman's consistent use of specific symbols such as sunglasses, which represent "a means by which a character can regulate the degree of his awareness by either choosing to wear them or not." Removing the glasses shows "not only an attempt at communication with another person, but that the gesture of revealing the naked eye leads to extreme vulnerability, so that the defences, the persona, must be restored as quickly as possible."[2] The author cites *Sorority Girl, Not of This Earth, X—The Man with the X-Ray Eyes,* and *The Tomb of Ligeia* in support of this idea.

Modern "criticism" of Corman follows the Di Franco-Naha line in fixing Corman's importance as an historical phenomenon rather than an artist, a creator. Thus we are as likely to see an article about him in *Forbes* magazine (21 December 1981) as in *Sight and Sound.* Corman's lack of acceptance as an artist is not helped by the fact that many of his films no longer exist as he shot them. Most of the meticulously color-designed, widescreen Poe films are now faded, or flat, or both. *I, Mobster, Naked Paradise,* and *Rock All Night,* on the other hand, appear to be lost films as of this writing.

Critical Rejection

An examination of Corman's films shows three primary reasons for the rejection of his work, even among intelligent critics such as Andrew Sarris and Georges Sadoul. The first of these is the widespread prejudice against low-budget films. Mainstream critics have generally ignored such films because of this "limitation." And those low-budget directors defended as artists—Joseph H. Lewis, Phil Karlson, and Edgar G. Ulmer—have been accepted because they in some way "redeemed" themselves from their low-budget origins. Ulmer, an undeniably brilliant artist, redeemed himself through the romantic notion of a "fall from grace," from the promise of his early associations with UFA, Max Reinhardt, Universal Studios, and his subsequent bitter toiling in Hollywood where he created masterworks like *Detour* that exhibit alternating strains of nihilism and romanticism. Unlike Ulmer, Corman did not suffer a fall; he started—and ended, as a director—working with low budget. Hence the romantic notion of estrangement from an institution that once accepted him—Hollywood, the magic world of the movies—does not apply to Corman.

Joseph H. Lewis and Phil Karlson typify the low-budget "action directors" who redeemed themselves through a native skill with actors, obtaining conventionally strong performances from their stars. They have also benefitted from their association with the cultishly popular genre of *film noir*, though in both cases they differ from Corman in covering a basic romantic orientation with the bitter overlay of *noir*. Certainly, John Dall and Peggy Cummins die at the end of Lewis's *Gun Crazy*, but their death is a romantic conception, the camera craning dramatically up and away from the couple, indicating a kind of triumph-in-death that lies at the heart of the romantic spirit.

Corman, on the other hand, is bluntly antiromantic, obsessively despairing in his manipulation of characters through hostile or meaningless environments. Whereas most directors are congratulated on the extent to which they can induce sympathy for their characters, Corman will build entire films (*Bucket of Blood, The St. Valentine's Day Massacre*) around unattractive, inchoate, even repellent characters. Corman's characters are not usually destroyed by society; their problems are interiorized and they destroy themselves, another strategy certain to alienate most critics, if not popular audiences. A Corman ending similar to that of Lewis's *Gun Crazy* is inconceivable; for his characters there is no triumph in death, only relief. Corman's nihilism is probably more thorough than any other director's, without the romantic or social alloy that would allow him (or us) to assign "blame" to others. Dr. Xavier's self-mutilation at the end of *X—The Man with the X-Ray Eyes* shows how far Corman is willing to go in positing a despairing view of life, and it is not an atypical film. The deterioration of the mind in the face of unanswerable questions—purpose, identity—exists in most of his films, in genres as diverse as comedy (*Bucket of Blood*), science fiction (*The Day the World Ended*), and certainly all the Poe films.

In addition to Corman's low-budget origins and his nihilism, there is the question of acting. In an otherwise complimentary blurb in *The Dictionary of Film Makers*, Georges Sadoul called the acting in Corman's films "rarely memorable," and much has been made of the wildly divergent acting styles evident in his films, from the so-called "camp" histrionics of Vincent Price to the method acting of Susan Cabot (*Machine Gun Kelly, Sorority Girl*), to the nonacting of people like Antony Carbone (*The Last Woman on Earth, The Pit and the Pendulum*). Corman's reluctance with actors is unquestionable; Boris Karloff, Robert Towne, Peter Bogdanovich, John Alonzo, and other collaborators have all commented on the director's "shyness" or "indifference" in trying to mold a performance. Since "acting" is one of the main avenues of critical approach to film (frequently with little distinction between classical stage acting styles and those required by the peculiar conventions of film), it is not surprising that Corman has been attacked for the "bad acting" in his films. While conventionally strong performances can be singled out (Charles Bronson in *Machine Gun Kelly* or William Shatner in *The Intruder*, for example), Corman's refusal to involve himself as much in the acting as in the other elements of his films becomes an important part of his aesthetic.

The characters who inhabit the world of his films exist randomly in a random, pointless universe. Corman's assumption of the godlike position of controlling from outside shows him primarily as creator of the ambience, the mood, the atmosphere in which these characters exist (e.g., the fog-enshrouded street in which *The Undead* opens), not in the generally static, unknowable personalities of the characters themselves. This is not to say that he does not "direct" them, since he must tell them when to talk, sometimes what to say, when to move, and when to stand still. But many of his characters are ciphers, mysterious personalities subordinated to the pervasive atmosphere of gloom and unfulfillment. Often the acting is extremely stylized (particularly in the Poe films), where the actor is simply another element hopelessly trapped in the director's complex, overripe mise-en-scène. In the Poe films, particularly, character is an extension, a manifestation, a prisoner, of environment. The overwhelming lushness of these films tends to supersede individual performances even by actors as powerful and mannered as Vincent Price or Peter Lorre. Boris Karloff confirmed, with uncharacteristic irritation, Corman's refusal to help him through a scene. According to Karloff, Corman said, "You're experienced actors, get on with it. I've got my lighting and my angles. I know how I'm going to put this together. . . . That's your pigeon. Go on. I'm busy with this."[3] Corman's countering comment shows the wide gulf between director and actor in this case: "They [actors like Price, Karloff, Lorre] all have this great ability of giving you all you can ask for and more. . . ."[4]

Frequently Corman splits the personality into two or more beings (*The Undead, War of the Satellites,* most of the Poe films), showing the utter mutability of the persona, its openness to manipulation and destruction. At other times, particularly in the early films, characters act according to archetypal or generic expectations (*The Day the World Ended, Teenage Caveman*), with Corman again, in a different way, closing off their options by making them victimized "types" rather than rounded, "believable" human beings.

His films abound with frustrated attempts by repressed characters to emerge, to live and breathe, to satisfy the demands of the ego to express itself. His most successful films—*The Pit and the Pendulum, X—The Man with the X-Ray Eyes, Masque of the Red Death*—augment the plot destruction of the characters with paradoxically organic images of repression: a woman's embrace evolves into a lethal Iron Maiden, the eyes that regulate consciousness become incapable of ever closing, a character's own face reappears as the face of death. In all cases, there is a reluctance on Corman's part to allow the emergence of the personality from the two-dimensional canvas of the film through the most striking pantomime of "real life"—acting.

Another reason for critical rejection of Corman lies in his attack on a foundational aspect of modern Western culture: patriarchy. This attack emerges in a variety of ways in Corman's films, most obviously in his use of weak, passive, impotent males as leads, and in his recasting of traditional male action pictures into "women's films," with women departing socially proscribed roles and assuming attitudes popularly conceived of as masculine. This is sometimes sugar-coated as absurdist comedy (*Viking Women and the Sea Serpent*), but more often dealt with in a curiously blunt way, with women outside the law engaging in physical assaults on men (*Swamp Women, Teenage Doll*), or controlling society from within (the sheriff and chief landowner in *The Gunslinger* are both women). Sometimes a woman manipulates a powerful man (*Machine Gun Kelly*), sometimes she kills him (*The Gunslinger, Tales of Terror, House of Usher*). In all these cases, the basic supposition of culture as a workable aggregate built on successful individual heterosexual couplings is challenged. Society's basic unit is portrayed as hopelessly unacceptable in the modern world—hence the departure of women from their limited, domestic world.

Corman's attack on patriarchy sometimes takes the form of religious parable (*Masque of the Red Death, X—The Man with the X-Ray Eyes*), with God the ultimate repressing patriarch. Patriarchy taken to its essence means simply death—the ultimate law of nature, God, the status quo. This is the most important factor in the lives of Corman's characters, particularly the men, and the one against which they create their own world which, unlike the real one, they can control, if only temporarily. Sometimes the "evil" influence of the past, of tainted bloodlines, is framed in a patriarchal mode—for example, *The Pit and the Pendulum*, in which Nicholas Medina's personality is so weak and fearful it is taken over by his father, who exists more strongly in Medina's mind than he himself does.

Corman's consistent return to this theme is marked not only in the Poe cycle, but in the gangster and outlaw films he made throughout the sixties. *The St. Valentine's Day Massacre, The Wild Angels,* and *Bloody Mama* document the attempts by a dissatisfied group to dismantle the patriarchy; at the same time, they show this group operating under many of the same rules noted in the dying patriarchal culture, hence they are equally doomed.

This concept exists even in Corman's less personal work, the films he produced for others, including much of the output of New World Pictures, the low-budget studio Corman owned during the 1970s. Not only were New World's films profeminist and antipatriarchal; even the foreign pickups for the company, at least in the early days, tended to be sex-role reversal-genre films—for example, *Frankenstein* becomes New World's *Lady Frankenstein,* the crime melodrama becomes *Stacy and Her Gangbusters.* Corman's claim that this frequent use of role-reversal was merely "a marketing decision" based on positive reception of films like *The Big Doll House* and *The Student Nurses* is belied by the fact that New World continued to reprise these themes long after their pioneering efforts in the genre had ceased to be very profitable (*TNT Jackson*), and the fact that when one female-dominated genre began to fade (e.g., women in prison), Corman usually invented another to take its place (e.g., the matriarchal rural chase films like *Big Bad Mama* and *Crazy Mama*).

Since film critics tend to reflect the values of their culture, consciously or not, Corman's relentless attacks on the culture, particularly in his hopeless, emphatically antiromantic and antipatriarchal view of humanity, could not be expected to arouse more than hostility or indifference among them.

The eventual reevaluation of Corman will occur through a closer reading of his films than has generally been the case. Corman's world-view emerges not only from his scripts, but also from his superior manipulation of the visual aspects of film: the editing, camera compositions and movements, set design, lighting, and acting. The fragile, achingly beautiful worlds of Roderick Usher or Prince Prospero or even Ma Barker in the idealized past are not the creations of words, but of intense color design, swirling camera movements, shock cuts, and montage sequences of great formal intensity. Corman's obsession with "putting the film together," his successful subordination of all other elements to the visual, resulted in the creation of not one, but many fantastic yet utterly convincing "alternate worlds"—some completely fabricated (the Poe films), some based on reality (*Bloody Mama*)—to the hopeless real one. Corman's modernist sensibility is confirmed by the fact that not only do his characters not achieve self-realization, they are usually destroyed in the attempt. Yet the hypnotic intensity of his rendering of the forbidden worlds created by his characters, which remain always just beyond their own grasp, makes them equally palpable to his audience (the Poe films have become a part of film legend), and Corman's vision will survive at the very least on this basis.

Notes and References

All uncredited quotes by Roger Corman are taken from interviews with Corman by the author in 1974 and 1982.

Chapter One

1. Bill Warren, *Keep Watching the Skies: American Science Fiction of the Fifties* (Jefferson, N.C.: McFarland & Co., 1982), 1:179.
2. Quoted in J. Philip Di Franco, *The Movie World of Roger Corman* (New York, 1979), 29.
3. Paul Willeman, David Pirie, David Will, and Lynda Myles, *Roger Corman: The Millennic Vision* (Edinburgh, Scotland, 1970), 27.
4. Quoted in Edmund Wilson, *Classics and Commercials* (New York: Farrar, Straus & Giroux, 1950), 290.

Chapter Two

1. Willeman, *Roger Corman*, 24.
2. Quoted in "The Pit and the Pen of Alex Gordon," *Fangoria* 3, no. 27 (1983): 35.
3. C. Jerry Kutner, personal communication.
4. Both quoted in Ed Naha, *The Films of Roger Corman: Brilliance on a Budget* (New York, 1982), 112.

Chapter Three

1. Willeman, *Roger Corman*, 25.
2. Ibid.
3. Ibid.
4. Quotes by Milton Krasner from "Recreating a Violent Era on Film for *The St. Valentine's Day Massacre*," *American Cinematographer*, October 1967, p. 706.
5. Naha, *Films of Roger Corman*, 186.
6. The most obvious example is George Segal shoving a sandwich into Jean Hale's face, as in the famous grapefruit scene in *Public Enemy*.
7. "Interview with Roger Corman," *Sight and Sound* 39 (Autumn 1970):183.

8.   Robert Warshow, "The Gangster as Tragic Hero," *Partisan Review* 15 (February 1948):243.

9.   Tom Milne, "Bloody Mama," *Sight and Sound* 39 (Autumn 1970):183.

10.   Interview with Roger Corman, 182.

Chapter Four

1.   Alberto Valvo, *Sight Restoration After Long-Term Blindness: The Problems and Behavior Patterns of Visual Rehabilitation* (New York: American Foundation for the Blind, 1971), 9.

2.   Willeman, *Roger Corman*, 27.

Chapter Five

1.   Two films, usually considered part of Corman's Poe cycle, are not discussed here. Space limitations did not permit an analysis of *Tales of Terror*, which, while far from being a failure, is probably the weakest of the series. The other film, *The Haunted Palace*, was based on an H. P. Lovecraft novel, *The Case of Charles Dexter Ward*, and has tenuous connections with the Poe universe.

2.   Herb A. Lightman, "A Study of Horror Film Photography," *American Cinematographer*, October 1961, p. 612.

3.   Jean-Loup Bourget, "Sirk and the Critics," *Bright Lights*, no. 6 (Winter 1975–76):10.

4.   In the 1950s, Corman generally used color in "outdoor" films (westerns, adventure stories), and black and white for the more interiorized "thrillers" (science fiction, horror, gangster films).

5.   Lightman, "A Study," 613.

6.   David Pirie, "Roger Corman's Descent into the Maelstrom," in *Roger Corman*, by Willeman, 52.

7.   C. Jerry Kutner, personal communication.

8.   Bevis Hillier, *Austerity/Binge: The Decorative Arts of the Forties and Fifties* (London: Studio Vista, 1975), 80.

9.   Willeman, *Roger Corman*, 61.

10.   Ibid.

11.   Ibid.

12.   Di Franco, *Movie World*, 116.

Chapter Six

1.   Warren, *Keep Watching the Skies*, 1:180.

2.   Willeman, *Roger Corman*, 27.

3.   John Brosnan, *Horror People* (New York: St. Martin's Press, 1976), 69.

4.   Boris Karloff, in *Sight and Sound* 32 (Winter 1963–64):132.

Selected Bibliography

Bonaparte, Marie. *The Life and Works of Edgar Allan Poe: A Psychoanalytic Interpretation.* London: Imago Publishing Co., 1949. Bonaparte's seminal work on Poe is currently out of favor with Poe scholars, but the text is invaluable in many ways, most particularly in isolating recurring motifs in his work and linking them to people and events in his life.

Di Franco, J. Philip, ed. *The Movie World of Roger Corman.* New York: Chelsea House Publishers, 1979. Though riddled with errors, this coffee-table book is valuable in giving firsthand information on production circumstances by Corman's collaborators on both sides of the camera.

Naha, Ed. *The Films of Roger Corman: Brilliance on a Budget.* New York: Arco Press, 1982. Slightly more ambitious than the previous work, Naha's book combines pop analysis with quotes from contemporary reviews.

Willeman, Paul, Pirie, David, Will, David, and **Myles, Lynda.** *Roger Corman: The Millennic Vision.* Edinburgh, Scotland: Edinburgh Film Festival, 1970. Unquestionably the most important and substantial criticism of Corman in English. Each of the essays is a model of its kind, but Willeman's in particular stands out as the definitive reading on Corman's themes.

Filmography

Unless otherwise noted, all films were produced and directed by Roger Corman. American-International Pictures is abbreviated to AIP, and Allied Artists to AA. Films with more complete credits are those discussed at length in the text.

FIVE GUNS WEST (AIP, 1955)
Screenplay: R. Wright Campbell; Photography: Floyd Crosby; Music: Buddy Bregman; Editor: Ronald Sinclair; Cast: John Lund, Dorothy Malone, Touch Connors, Paul Birch, James Stone. Running Time: 78 mins.

APACHE WOMAN (AIP, 1955)
Screenplay: Lou Rusoff; Photography: Floyd Crosby; Music: Ronald Stein; Editor: Ronald Sinclair; Sound: Herman Lewis; Cast: Lloyd Bridges, Joan Taylor, Lance Fuller, Morgan Jones, Paul Birch, Lou Place. Running Time: 82 mins.

THE DAY THE WORLD ENDED (AIP, 1955)
Screenplay: Lou Rusoff; Photography: Jock Feindel; Music: Ronald Stein; Editor: Ronald Sinclair; Sound: James Speak; Cast: Richard Denning (Rick), Lori Nelson (Louise), Adele Jergens (Ruby), Touch Connors (Tony), Paul Birch (Maddison), Raymond Hatton (Pete), Paul Dubov (Radek), Jonathan Haze (Contaminated Man), Paul Blaisdell (Mutant). Running Time: 78 mins.

SWAMP WOMEN (AIP, 1955)
Producer: Bernard Woolner; Screenplay: David Stern; Photography: Fred West; Music: Willis Holman; Editor: Ronald Sinclair; Cast: Beverly Garland, Carole Matthews, Touch Connors, Marie Windsor, Jill Jarmyn. Running Time: 70 mins.

THE OKLAHOMA WOMAN (AIP, 1955)
Screenplay: Lou Rusoff; Photography: Fred West; Music: Ronald Stein; Editor: Ronald Sinclair; Cast: Richard Denning, Peggie Castle, Cathy Downs, Tudor Owens, Martin Kingsley, Touch Connors. Running Time: 71 mins.

THE GUNSLINGER (AIP, 1956)
Screenplay: Charles B. Griffith and Mark Hanna; Photography: Fred West; Music: Ronald Stein; Editor: Charles Gross, Jr.; Art Director: Harry Reif; Cast: John Ireland, Beverly Garland, Allison Hayes, Martin Kingsley, Jonathan Haze, Chris Alcaide. Running Time: 76 mins.

IT CONQUERED THE WORLD (AIP, 1956)
Screenplay: Lou Rusoff; Photography: Fred West; Music: Ronald Stein; Sound: Phil Mitchell; Cast: Peter Graves, Beverly Garland, Lee van Cleef, Sally Fraser, Charles B. Griffith, Dick Miller, Jonathan Haze, Russ Bender, Paul Blaisdell. Running Time: 68 mins.

NOT OF THIS EARTH (AA, 1956)
Screenplay: Charles B. Griffith and Mark Hanna; Photography: John Mescall; Music: Ronald Stein; Editor: Charles Gross, Jr.; Sound: Philip Mitchell; Cast: Paul Birch (Paul Johnson), Beverly Garland (Nadine Storey), Morgan Jones (Harry Sherbourne), William Roerick (Dr. Rochelle), Jonathan Haze (Jeremy Perrin), Dick Miller (Joe Piper), Ann Carroll (Davanna Woman), Pat Flynn (Simmons), Tamar Cooper (Joanne), Gail Ganley (Girl). Running Time: 67 mins.

THE UNDEAD (AA, 1956)
Screenplay: Charles B. Griffith and Mark Hanna; Photography: William Sickner; Music: Ronald Stein; Editor: Frank Sullivan; Sound: Bob Post; Cast: Pamela Duncan, Richard Garland, Allison Hayes, Val DuFour, Mel Welles, Dorothy Neuman, Billy Barty, Richard Devon. Running Time: 71 mins.

THE SHE GODS OF SHARK REEF (AIP, 1956)
Producer: Ludwig Gerber; Screenplay: Robert Hill and Victor Stoloff; Photography: Floyd Crosby; Music: Ronald Stein; Editor: Frank Sullivan; Sound: Bob Post; Cast: Don Durant, Bill Cord, Lisa Montell, Jeanne Gerson, Carol Lindsay, Beverly Rivera. Running Time: 63 mins.

NAKED PARADISE (AIP, 1956)
Screenplay: Charles B. Griffith and Mark Hanna; Photography: Floyd Crosby; Music: Ronald Stein; Editor: Charles Gross, Jr.; Sound: Bob Post; Cast: Richard Denning, Beverly Garland, Lisa Montell, Leslie Bradley, Dick Miller, Jonathan Haze. Running Time: 68 mins.

ATTACK OF THE CRAB MONSTERS (AA, 1956)
Screenplay: Charles B. Griffith; Photography: Floyd Crosby; Music: Ronald Stein; Editor: Charles Gross, Jr.; Sound: Bob Post; Cast: Richard Garland (Dale Drewer), Pamela Duncan (Martha Hunter), Russell Johnson (Hank Chapman), Leslie Bradley (Dr. Karl Weingard), Richard Cutting (Dr. James Carson), Mel Welles (Jules Deveroux), Beech Dickerson (Ron Fellows), Tony Miller (Jack Sommers), Ed Nelson (Ensign Quinlan). Running Time: 62 mins.

ROCK ALL NIGHT (AIP, 1956)
Screenplay: Charles B. Griffith, from a story by David P. Harman;
Photography: Floyd Crosby; Music: Buck Ram; Editor: Frank Sullivan;
Sound: Bob Post; Art Director: Robert Kinoshita; Cast: Dick Miller, Abby
Dalton, Robin Morse, Richard Cutting, Bruno Ve Sota, Chris Alcaide, Mel
Welles, Barboura Morris, The Platters. Running Time: 70 mins.

TEENAGE DOLL (AA, 1957)
Screenplay: Charles B. Griffith; Photography: Floyd Crosby; Music: Walter
Greene; Editor: Charles Gross, Jr.; Sound: Bob Post; Art Director: Robert
Kinoshita; Cast: June Kenney (Barbara), Fay Spain (Hel), John Brinkley
(Eddie), Colette Jackson (May), Barbara Wilson (Betty), Ziva Rodan
(Squirrel), Sandy Smith (Lorrie), Barboura Morris (Janet), Richard Devon
(Dunston), Jay Sayer (Wally), Richard Cutting (Phil), Dorothy Neuman
(Estelle), Ed Nelson (Dutch Doctor). Running Time: 67 minutes.

CARNIVAL ROCK (AIP, 1957)
Screenplay: Leo Lieberman; Photography: Floyd Crosby; Music: Walter
Greene and Buck Ram; Editor: Charles Gross, Jr.; Sound: Bob Post; Art
Director: Robert Kinoshita; Cast: Susan Cabot, Brian Hutton, David J.
Stewart, Dick Miller, Iris Adrian, Jonathan Haze, Ed Nelson, Chris Alcaide.
Running Time: 75 mins.

SORORITY GIRL (AIP, 1957)
Screenplay: Ed Waters and Leo Lieberman; Photography: Monroe P. Askins;
Music: Ronald Stein; Editor: Charles Gross, Jr.; Sound: Bob Post; Cast:
Susan Cabot, Dick Miller, Barboura Morris, June Kenney, Barbara Crane,
Fay Baker, Jeanne Wood. Running Time: 61 mins.

THE VIKING WOMEN AND THE SEA SERPENT (AIP, 1957)
Screenplay: Louis Goldman; Photography: Monroe P. Askins; Music: Albert
Glasser; Editor: Ronald Sinclair; Sound: Herman Lewis; Art Director:
Robert Kinoshita; Cast: Abby Dalton, Susan Cabot, Brad Jackson, June
Kenney, Richard Devon, Betsy Jones-Moreland, Jonathan Haze, Jay Sayer.
Running Time: 66 mins.

WAR OF THE SATELLITES (AA, 1957)
Screenplay: Louis Goldman, from a story by Irving Block and Jack Rabin;
Photography: Floyd Crosby; Music: Walter Greene; Editor: Irene Morra;
Sound: Philip Mitchell; Art Director: Daniel Haller; Cast: Susan Cabot,
Richard Devon, Dick Miller, Robert Shayne, Jerry Barclay, Mitzi McCall,
Eric Sinclair. Running Time: 66 mins.

MACHINE GUN KELLY (AIP, 1958)
Screenplay: R. Wright Campbell; Photography: Floyd Crosby (Superscope);
Music: Gerald Fried; Editor: Ronald Sinclair; Sound: Ryder Sound Service;
Art Director: Daniel Haller; Cast: Charles Bronson (Machine Gun Kelly),

Susan Cabot (Flo), Morey Amsterdam (Fandango), Jack Lambert (Howard), Wally Campo (Maize), Bob Griffin (Vito), Barboura Morris (Lynn), Richard Devon (Apple), Ted Thorpe (Teddy), Mitzi McCall (Harriet), Frank De Kova (Harry), Connie Gilchrist (Ma), Jay Sayer (Philip Ashton), Shirley Falls (Martha). Running Time: 83 mins.

TEENAGE CAVEMAN (AIP, 1958)
Screenplay: R. Wright Campbell; Photography: Floyd Crosby; Music: Al Glasser; Editor: Irene Morra; Sound: Philip Mitchell; Cast: Robert Vaughn, Leslie Bradley, Darah Marshall, Frank De Kova, Joseph Hamilton, Marshal Bradford, Robert Shayne. Running Time: 65 mins.

I, MOBSTER (Twentieth Century-Fox, 1958)
Screenplay: Steve Fisher, from the novel by J. H. Smyth; Photography: Floyd Crosby; Music: Gerald Fried and Ed L. Alperson; Editor: William B. Murphy; Sound: Philip Mitchell; Art Director: Daniel Haller; Cast: Steve Cochran, Lita Milan, Robert Strauss, Celia Lovsky, Lili St. Cyr, Jeri Southern, John Brinkley, Yvette Vickers, Grant Withers. Running Time: 80 mins.

A BUCKET OF BLOOD (AIP, 1959)
Screenplay: Charles B. Griffith; Photography: Jack Marquette; Music: Fred Katz; Editor: Anthony Carras; Sound: Wally Nogle and Leonard Corso; Art Director: Daniel Haller; Cast: Dick Miller (Walter Paisley), Barboura Morris (Carla), Antony Carbone (Leonard), Julian Burton (Max Brock), Ed Nelson (Art Lacroix), John Brinkley (Will), John Shaner (Oscar), Judy Bamber (Alice), Myrtle Domerel (Mrs. Swickert), Bert Convy (Lou Raby), Jhean Burton (Naolia). Running Time: 66 mins.

THE WASP WOMAN (AIP, 1959)
Screenplay: Leo Cordon, from a story by Kinta Zertuche; Photography: Harry C. Newman; Music: Fred Katz; Editor: Carlo Lodato; Art Director: Daniel Haller; Cast: Susan Cabot, Fred Eiseley, Barboura Morris, Michael Marks, William Roerick. Running Time: 66 mins.

SKI TROOP ATTACK (Filmgroup, 1960)
Screenplay: Charles B. Griffith; Photography: Andy Costikyan; Music: Fred Katz; Editor: Anthony Carras; Cast: Frank Wolff, Michael Forest, Wally Campo, Richard Sinatra, Sheila Carol, Roger Corman. Running Time: 63 mins.

THE FALL OF THE HOUSE OF USHER (AIP, 1960)
Screenplay: Richard Matheson, from the story by E. A. Poe; Photography: Floyd Crosby (Cinemascope); Music: Les Baxter; Editor: Anthony Carras; Sound: Philip Mitchell; Art Director: Daniel Haller; Paintings: Burt Schoenberg; Cast: Vincent Price (Roderick Usher), Mark Damon (Philip Winthrop), Myrna Fahey (Madeleine Usher), Harry Ellerbe (Bristol).

Ghosts: Bill Borzage, Mike Jordan, Nadajan, Ruth Oklander, George Paul, David Andar, Eleanor Le Faber, Geraldine Paulette, Phil Sylvestre, John Zimeas. Running Time: 80 mins.

THE LITTLE SHOP OF HORRORS (AIP, 1960)
Screenplay: Charles B. Griffith; Photography: Arch Dalzell; Music: Fred Katz; Editor: Marshall Neilan, Jr.; Art Director: Daniel Haller; Cast: Jonathan Haze, Jackie Joseph, Mel Welles, Myrtle Vail, Dick Miller, Leola Wendorff, Jack Nicholson. Running Time: 70 mins.

THE LAST WOMAN ON EARTH (Filmgroup, 1960)
Screenplay: Ed Wain (Robert Towne); Photography: Jack Marquette; Music: Ronald Stein; Editor: Anthony Carras; Sound: Beech Dickerson; Cast: Antony Carbone, Betsy Jones-Moreland, Edward Wain (Robert Towne). Running Time: 71 mins.

CREATURE FROM THE HAUNTED SEA (Filmgroup, 1960)
Screenplay: Charles B. Griffith; Photography: Jacques Marquette; Music: Fred Katz; Editor: Angela Scellars; Cast: Antony Carbone, Betsy Jones-Moreland, Edward Wain (Robert Towne), E. R. Alvarez, Robert Bean, Sonya Noemi. Running Time: 63 mins.

ATLAS (Filmgroup, 1960)
Screenplay: Charles B. Griffith; Photography: Basil Maros; Music: Ronald Stein; Editor: Michael Luciano; Sound: Allen Herschey; Cast: Michael Forest, Frank Wolff, Barboura Morris, Walter Maslow, Christos Exarchos, Andreas Filippidis. Running Time: 79 mins.

THE PIT AND THE PENDULUM (AIP, 1961)
Screenplay: Richard Matheson, from the story by E. A. Poe; Photography: Floyd Crosby (Panavision); Music: Les Baxter; Editor: Anthony Carras; Sound: Roy Meadows; Art Director: Daniel Haller; Cast: Vincent Price (Nicholas Medina), John Kerr (Francis Barnard), Barbara Steele (Elizabeth), Luana Anders (Catherine Medina), Antony Carbone (Dr. Charles Leon), Patrick Westwood (Maximillian), Lynne Bernay (Maria), Larry Turner (Nicholas as a child), Mary Menzies (Isabella), Charles Victor (Bartolome). Running Time: 85 mins.

THE INTRUDER (Pathe-American, 1961)
Screenplay: Charles Beaumont, adapted from his novel; Photography: Taylor Byars (uncredited: Haskell Wexler); Music: Ronald Stein; Editor: Ronald Sinclair; Sound: John Bury; Production Manager: Jack Bohrer; Filmed on location in Missouri; Cast: William Shatner (Adam Cramer), Frank Maxwell (Tom McDaniel), Beverly Lunsford (Ella McDaniel), Robert Emhardt (Verne Shipman), Jeanne Cooper (Vi), Leo Gordon (Sam Griffin), Charles Barnes (Joey Green), Charles Beaumont (Dr. Harley Paton), Katherine Smith (Ruth McDaniel). Running Time: 84 mins. Also released as *Shame* (1966) and *I Hate Your Guts*.

THE PREMATURE BURIAL (AIP, 1961)
Screenplay: Charles Beaumont and Ray Russell, from the story by E. A. Poe; Photography: Floyd Crosby (Panavision); Music: Ronald Stein; Editor: Ronald Sinclair; Sound: John Bury; Art Director: Daniel Haller; Cast: Ray Milland (Guy Carrell), Hazel Court (Emily Gault), Richard Ney (Miles Archer), Heather Angel (Kate Carrell), Alan Napier (Dr. Gideon Gault), John Dierkes (Sweeney), Richard Miller (Mole), Brendon Dillon (Minister). Running Time: 81 mins.

TALES OF TERROR (AIP, 1961)
Screenplay: Richard Matheson, "Morella," "The Black Cat," and "The Facts in the Case of M. Valdemar," by E. A. Poe; Photography: Floyd Crosby (Panavision); Music: Les Baxter; Editor: Anthony Carras; Sound: Jack Woods; Art Director: Daniel Haller; Cast: Vincent Price, Peter Lorre, Basil Rathbone, Debra Paget, Maggie Pierce, Leona Gage, Joyce Jameson, Wally Campo. Running Time: 88 mins.

TOWER OF LONDON (United Artists, 1962)
Producer: Gene Corman; Screenplay: Leo Gordon, James B. Gordon and Amos Powell, from a story by Leo Gordon and Amos Powell; Photography: Arch Dalzell; Editor: Ronald Sinclair; Music: Michael Anderson; Art Director: Daniel Haller; Cast: Vincent Price, Michael Pate, Joan Freeman, Robert Brown, Justice Watson, Sara Selby. Running Time: 79 mins.

THE YOUNG RACERS (AIP 1962)
Screenplay: R. Wright Campbell; Photography: Floyd Crosby; Music: Les Baxter; Editor: Ronald Sinclair; Sound: Francis Ford Coppola; Art Director: Albert Locatelli; Cast: Mark Damon, William Campbell, Luana Anders, Robert Campbell, Patrick Magee, Milo Quesada. Running Time: 82 mins.

THE RAVEN (AIP, 1962)
Screenplay: Richard Matheson, from the poem by E. A. Poe; Photography: Floyd Crosby (Panavision); Music: Les Baxter; Editor: Ronald Sinclair; Sound: John Bury; Art Director: Daniel Haller; Cast: Vincent Price (Craven), Peter Lorre (Dr. Bedlo), Jack Nicholson (Rexford), Boris Karloff (Scarabus), Hazel Court (Lenore), Olive Sturgess (Estelle), Jim, Jr. (The Raven). Running Time: 86 mins.

THE TERROR (AIP, 1962)
Screenplay: Leo Gordon and Jack Hill; Photography: John Nickolaus, Music: Ronald Stein; Editor: Stuart O'Brien; Sound: John Bury; Art Director: Daniel Haller; Cast: Boris Karloff, Jack Nicholson, Sandra Knight, Dick Miller, Dorothy Neuman, Jonathan Haze. Running Time: 81 mins.

X—THE MAN WITH THE X-RAY EYES (AIP, 1963)
Screenplay: Robert Dillon and Ray Russell, from a story by Russell; Photography: Floyd Crosby (Panavision); Music: Les Baxter; Editor: Anthony Carrass; Sound: Al Bird; Art Director: Daniel Haller; Cast: Ray Milland (Dr.

James Xavier), Diana Van der Vlis (Dr. Diane Fairfax), Harold J. Stone (Dr.
Sam Brant), John Hoyt (Dr. Willard Benson), Don Rickles (Crane), John
Dierkes (Preacher), Lorrie Summers (Party Dancer), Vickie Lee (Girl
Patient), Kathryn Hart (Mrs. Mart), Dick Miller (Boy at Fairground).
Running Time: 80 mins.

THE HAUNTED PALACE (AIP, 1963)
Screenplay: Charles Beaumont, from the poem by E. A. Poe and a novel by
H. P. Lovecraft; Photography: Floyd Crosby; Music: Ronald Stein; Editor:
Ronald Sinclair; Art Director: Daniel Haller; Cast: Vincent Price, Debra
Paget, Lon Chaney, Jr., John Dierkes, Leo Gordon, Elisha Cook, Frank
Maxwell. Running Time: 87 mins.

THE SECRET INVASION (United Artists, 1963)
Producer: Gene Corman; Screenplay: R. Wright Campbell; Photography:
Arthur E. Arling; Music: Hugo Friedhofer; Editor: Ronald Sinclair; Sound:
Gene Corso; Art Director: John Murray; Cast: Stewart Granger, Raf Vallone,
Mickey Rooney, Edd Byrnes, Henry Silva, Mia Massini, William Campbell.
Running Time: 95 mins.

THE MASQUE OF THE RED DEATH (AIP, 1964)
Screenplay: Charles Beaumont and R. Wright Campbell, from the story by
R. Wright Campbell; Photography: Nicolas Roeg (Panavision); Music: David
Lee; Editor: Ann Chegwidden; Sound: Richard Bird and Len Abbott; Art
Director: Daniel Haller; Choreography: Jack Carter; Cast: Vincent Price
(Prince Prospero), Hazel Court (Juliana), Jane Asher (Francesca), David
Weston (Gino), Patrick Magee (Alfredo), Nigel Green (Ludovico), Skip
Martin (Hop Toad), John Westbrook (Man in Red), Gay Brown (Senora
Escobar), Julian Burton (Senor Escobar), Doreen Dawn (Anna-Marie), Paul
Whitsun-Jones (Scarlatti), Jean Lodge (Scarlatti's wife), Verina Greenlaw
(Esmeralda), Brian Hewlett (Lampredi), Harvey Hall (Clistor). Running
Time: 89 mins.

THE TOMB OF LIGEIA (AIP, 1964)
Screenplay: Robert Towne, from the story by E. A. Poe, Photography:
Arthur Grant (Colorscope); Music: Kenneth V. Jones; Editor: Alfred Cox;
Sound: Les Wiggins and Don Ranasinghe; Art Director: Colin Southcott;
Cast: Vincent Price (Verden Fell), Elizabeth Shephard (Rowena/Ligeia), John
Westbrook (Christopher Gough), Oliver Johnston (Kenrick), Derek Francis
(Lord Trevanion), Richard Vernon (Dr. Vivian), Ronald Adam (Parson), Frank
Thornton (Peperel), Denis Gilmore (Livery Boy). Running Time: 81 mins.

THE WILD ANGELS (AIP, 1966)
Screenplay: Charles B. Griffith; Photography: Richard Moore; Music: Mike
Curb; Editor: Monte Hellman; Sound: Philip Mitchell; Art Director: Leon
Ericksen; Cast: Peter Fonda, Nancy Sinatra, Bruce Dern, Diane Ladd, Buck
Taylor, Lou Procopio, Coby Denton, Marc Cavell. Running Time: 82 mins.

THE ST. VALENTINE'S DAY MASSACRE (Twentieth Century-Fox, 1966)
Screenplay: Howard Browne; Photography: Milton Krasner (Cinemascope);
Music: Fred Steiner; Editor: William B. Murphy; Sound: Herman Lewis and
David Dockendorf; Art Directors: Jack Martin Smith and Philip Jeffries;
Narrator: Paul Frees; Cast: Jason Robards (Al Capone), George Segal (Peter
Gusenberg), Ralph Meeker (Bugs Moran), Jean Hale (Myrtle), Clint Ritchie
(Jack McGurn), Frank Silvera (Sorello), Michele Guayini (Patsy Lelordo),
Joseph Campanella (Weinshank), Richard Bakalyan (Scalisi), David Canary
(Frank Gusenberg), Bruce Dern (May), Harold J. Stone (Frank Nitti), Kurt
Kreuger (James Clark), Paul Richards (Charles Fischetti), Joseph Turkel
(Guzik), Leo Gordon (Heitler), Milton Frome (Adam Heyer), Mickey Deems
(Schwimmer), John Agar (O'Bannion), Celia Lovsky (Josephine Schwimmer),
Reed Hadley (Hymie Weiss), Alex D'Arcy (Aiello), Charles Dierkop
(Salvanti), Alex Rocco (Diamond), Betsy Jones-Moreland (Reporter),
Barboura Morris (Screaming Woman). Running Time: 99 mins.

THE TRIP (AIP, 1967)
Screenplay: Jack Nicholson; Photography: Arch Dalzell; Music: performed by
the Electric Flag; Editor: Ronald Sinclair; Sound: Philip Mitchell; Costumes:
Richard Bruno; Cast: Peter Fonda (Paul), Susan Strasberg (Sally), Bruce
Dern (John), Dennis Hopper (Max), Salli Sasche (Glenn), Katherine Walsh
(Lulu), Barboura Morris (Flo), Caren Bernsen (Alexandra), Dick Miller
(Cash), Luana Anders (Waitress), Tommy Signorelli (Al), Mitzi Hoag (Wife),
Peter Bogdanovich (Cameraman), Brandon de Wilde (Assistant Director).
Running Time: 83 mins.

BLOODY MAMA (AIP, 1970)
Screenplay: Robert Thom, from a story by Robert Thom and Don Peters;
Photography: John Alonzo; Music: Don Randi; Editor: Eve Newman; Sound:
Charles Knight; Special Effects: A. D. Flowers; Cast: Shelley Winters (Ma
Barker), Pat Hingle (Sam Pendlebury), Don Stroud (Herman Barker), Diane
Varsi (Mona Gibson), Bruce Dern (Kevin Dirkman), Clint Kimbrough
(Arthur Barker), Alex Nicol (George Barker), Michael Fox (Dr. Roth),
Scatman Crothers (Moses), Robert De Niro (Lloyd Barker), Pamela Dunlop
(Rembrandt). Running Time: 90 mins.

GAS-S-S-S, or, IT BECAME NECESSARY TO DESTROY THE WORLD
IN ORDER TO SAVE IT (AIP, 1970)
Screenplay: George Armitage; Photography: Ron Dexter; Editor: George Van
Noy; Art Director: David Nichols; Music: Country Joe and the Fish; Sound:
James Tannenbaum; Cast: Robert Corff, Elaine Giftos, Bud Cort, Talia
Coppola (Shire), Ben Vereen, Cindy Williams, Alex Wilson, Lou Procopio,
Phil Borneo, Jackie Farley. Running Time: 79 mins.

VON RICHTHOFEN AND BROWN (United Artists, 1970)
Producer: Gene Corman; Screenplay: John and Joyce Carrington;
Photography: Michael Reed; Music: Hugo Friedhofer; Editors: George Van

Noy and Alan Collins; Art Director: Jim Murakami; Cast: John Phillip Law,
Don Stroud, Barry Primus, Karen Huston, Corin Redgrave, Hurd Hatfield,
Peter Masterson. Running Time: 97 mins.

Note on Rental and Purchase

Most of Corman's films are available for 16mm rental. The most complete single source is Films Incorporated, whose catalog includes *The
Day the World Ended, Bucket of Blood*, and the entire Poe series,
including the last two still available in Cinemascope/Panavision (*The
House of Usher* and *Tales of Terror*). Films Incorporated is located at
440 Park Avenue South, New York, NY 10016.

The rights to three of the films discussed here—*Not of This Earth,
Attack of the Crab Monsters*, and *Teenage Doll*—recently reverted to
Corman, though they should eventually be available for rental again.

An increasing number of Corman's films are obtainable for sale or
rent on videotape, Beta or VHS. These include *House of Usher, The
Pit and the Pendulum, The Raven, Tales of Terror*, and *Masque of the
Red Death*, all from Warner Home Video. Cumberland Video (Suite
104, 3917 W. Riverside Drive, Burbank, CA 91505) sells these, as well
as *The Trip, Bloody Mama, X—The Man with the X-Ray Eyes*, and
The Wild Angels.

Index